JUST LIKE MAMA
USED TO MAKE

Lella Antinozzi

Lella Antinozzi

RECIPES AND TRADITIONS FROM AN ITALIAN KITCHEN

photography by Floris Leeuwenberg

Notes to the recipes:

1. Standard level spoon measurements are used in all recipes.

> *1 tablespoon = 15ml*
>
> *1 teaspoon = 5ml*

2. Both imperial and metric measurements are given in all recipes. Use one set of measurements only and not a mixture of both.

3. Eggs are medium unless otherwise stated. This book contains dishes made with raw or lightly cooked eggs. It is prudent for more vulnerable people, such as pregnant and nursing mothers, invalids, the elderly, babies, and young children, to avoid uncooked or lightly cooked dishes made with eggs. Once prepared, these dishes should be kept refrigerated and used promptly.

4. Milk is whole unless otherwise stated.

5. Fresh herbs are used unless otherwise stated. If they are unavailable, use dried herbs as an alternative but halve the quantity given.

6. Ovens should be preheated to the specified temperature. If using a fan-assisted oven, follow the manufacturer's directions for adjusting the time and the temperature.

7. Many of the recipes in this book require the use of type "0" pasta flour. This is widely available in Italy and may be purchased outside Italy in some supermarkets and delicatessens. If you cannot obtain it, Italian "00" flour can be used instead.

First published in Great Britain in 2005 by Cassell Illustrated,
a division of Octopus Publishing Group Limited
2–4 Heron Quays, London E14 4JP

Distributed in the United States of America by
Sterling Publishing Co., Inc.,
387 Park Avenue South, New York, NY 10016-8810

A CIP catalogue record for this book is available from the British Library.

ISBN 1 84403 429 1
EAN 9781844034291

Design by Riccardo Burgio
Translated by Jane Griffiths
Publishing Manager Anna Cheifetz
Art Director Auberon Hedgecoe

Printed in China

CONTENTS

Jammocenne ind'a 'a cucina
(Local dialect for "Let's go into the kitchen")
Camillo

INTRODUCTION

Italian mothers, or at least the traditional ones, are famous for being particularly attentive to the aspects of living that are connected with food. Their sometimes overprotective warmth and total devotion to the stove and to feeding their family have made them symbolic figures. So it's only natural that an Italian mama's recipe book, like this one, contains within itself the story of an entire life.

THREE GENERATIONS IN THE KITCHEN

Who is Mamma Rosetta?

Mamma Rosetta really exists. Like many other mothers in Italy, particularly in the South, she has a comfortably well-rounded figure and spends most of her time in the kitchen. For more than 40 years, she has been married to Papà Carmine, whom we call Papino (which means "Daddy"), and they are still very much in love.

Each afternoon, Papino brings Donna Rosa, as he calls her, a fresh rose that he has picked on his afternoon walk. They have lived in Rome since they married, but they come from two villages a little over five miles (eight kilometers) away from each other in the province of Caserta, not far from Naples. They've kept one thing in particular from their native countryside: a love of real food. The love and passion which Mamma Rosetta brings to her cooking are strengthened by a deep connection with her roots.

Nobody forces Mamma Rosetta to be in her kitchen, but there's nothing to be done about it. Her first thought in the morning is what to cook for lunch, or that evening, or for lunch the next day, or the day after that. There's always something to be done in the kitchen. That's the way it's always been with her, so of course Mamma Rosetta's recipe book is full to bursting with recipes of every type collected over many years.

The characters

Zia Carmela

Mamma Rosetta learned to cook from an elderly aunt known as Zia Carmela, who had been busy at the stove since she was a small child. Zia Carmela carried on cooking without ever stopping, until she reached the great age of 87. She in her turn had learned from Rosetta's grandmother, Nonna Rosa, and so on, generation after generation.

Zia Carmela never married. This was a long story, which she never told in detail. So it was, since she didn't have a family of her own and she loved to cook, that when her mother died she went to live in her brother Antonio's house. He had a fine family—he and Donna Assunta had five children, including our Rosetta. Zia Carmela looked after the cooking, and since Rosetta wanted to learn, she was happy to teach.

The land

The culinary tradition that fostered these women was that of the farmers in a very fertile area known as the *Terra di lavoro*, in the province of Caserta, near the river Garigliano, which forms the boundary between the regions of Lazio and Campania. In this area, the values of the land are deeply rooted and food and eating together are of central importance.

Nonno Antonio Lato

My grandfather Nonno Antonio, for example, always enjoyed having a meal with a crowd of friends. Don Antonio Lato's home in San Clemente di Galluccio was always full of people: there'd be the village mayor, the parish priest, the local sergeant, the doctor, a friend who went walking with him, and a new guest.

Anyone who happened to turn up at lunchtime had no choice but to stop. You can easily imagine that with five children in the family, they needed a hand in the kitchen.

Making herself busy

Even when she was only five or six, Rosetta was often given the task of decanting the wine in the cellar. It seems that she liked doing this very much, particularly in the summer, when it was the coolest part of the house. She also liked it because the wine was siphoned using a rubber tube and required a first sip to pass it from the barrel to the bottle.

It goes without saying that once Rosetta had had a few sips, she felt perfectly entitled to go and give the guests her opinion about the procedure, standing in the middle of the half-cleared table at the end of the midday meal. She felt it was her duty to make little speeches. It seems that they all found the soliloquies of Rosetta, the tipsy little girl, very amusing.

Stories and legends

What Rosetta certainly didn't know was that Dionysus himself, the god of wine, had introduced the first vines only a few miles away. By good fortune, San Clemente di Galluccio, the village where the women who wrote our recipes were born, was very close to the land known to the ancient Romans as the *Ager Falernus*—the source of Falernian wine, the most famous wine of ancient times. Falernian wine was served at all the best dinner tables in Rome; Horace, Cicero, Livy, Martial, and many, many others got drunk on it.

In reality, it seems that it was the Greeks of Thessaly who introduced viniculture to the region in the eighth century BC. This nectar was so divine, however, that people liked to think that it had been created through the direct intervention of Dionysus. Legend has it that Dionysus was the guest of an old man called Falernus, in a hut on the slopes of Monte Massico, between Sessa Aurunca and Mondragone. Out of gratitude for his hospitality, Dionysus granted Falernus fields of flourishing vines.

A philosophy of life

It goes without saying, then, that no meal was complete without wine! Not too much, just two or three glasses with each meal, but there would have been trouble if there wasn't any.

No one even started eating without a glass of wine, because that would have meant drinking water, which was regarded as scarcely fit to drink at table. "Water rots ships," Nonna Assunta used to say, and if she'd had one too many she'd comfort herself by saying, "Better drunk than ill." There was the warm and happy atmosphere, lively even, that you get with people who love to enjoy the pleasures of the table in good company.

Wine, oil, preserves, vinegar, lard, sausages, brawn, bread, pizza, and everything else were all made at home. Following the timeless wisdom that has been passed from mother to daughter, our recipe book is a distillation of popular culture and much else besides.

Nonna Assunta Affronte

Zia Carmela always consulted with Nonna Assunta before deciding on the menu for that day or for a feast day. Nonna Assunta also enjoyed fine food and good company—so much so that once she had reached a certain age, she could boast a considerable bulk. If anyone pointed out the notable size of her posterior, she, being very tall, countered with a reply that has become a well-known saying in our family: "Well, it's obvious that a big house like this needed a big entrance!"

Nonna Assunta came from Gaeta, a seaport and fishing town, so she was almost a Neapolitan, which you could tell because as soon as she opened her mouth she had something witty to say. She always managed to find the right proverb or phrase at the right moment, and often used metaphors from the kitchen. For example, if someone wouldn't take anyone else's views on board, she would retort: "Octopus is cooked in its own liquor." If someone else talked too much without eating anything, she would remind us that "Words don't fill the belly."

Like any good Neapolitan from Gaeta, she was mad about the lottery and there was only one thing that she could never have accepted—spending a Christmas Eve without *"o capitone ch' 'e recchie"* (a large eel, which is a seasonal delicacy in Campania—see recipe, page 133).

Why was Gaeta Neapolitan?

Nonna Assunta was born on April 3 1900—just 40 years after the last King of Naples, Francesco II, known to the Neapolitans as "Franceschiello," had escaped from Garibaldi and taken refuge in Gaeta with his wife Maria Sofia and his faithful courtiers.

It was the last bastion of hope for the Bourbons over many long months. Nonna Assunta had a great many tales to tell about the flight of Franceschiello and Donna Sofia. One of them—the funniest—was about a conversation between the king and queen. Donna Sofia wanted her husband to go back to Naples, but he no longer had any armed forces—only his bodyguards and some courtiers.

Donna Sofia hadn't given up and simply couldn't understand why her husband, the king, did nothing to oppose Garibaldi's advance. Franceschiello, who couldn't stand her grumbling any longer, said, "Donna Sofi, sometimes men are born into this world who are such fools that God in his mercy, to save them from starvation, makes them kings!"

Gaeta

Gaeta is a pleasant seaside town with small white houses looking out over a gulf that has become famous for its beauty—a paradise on the coastline of Lazio, just before the border with Campania. As part of the kingdom of Naples, it was always a strategically important naval base.

In Gaeta, people spoke a thick Neapolitan dialect and ate Neapolitan food; in short, it was a real outpost of Naples. Nonna Assunta was born in via Guastaferri, in the heart of the old town, and Nonno Antonio, who was from San Clemente, worked opposite her home. That's how they met and fell in love. After their marriage, they went to live in the hills inland, in San Clemente, and Nonna Assunta brought all her "Neapolitanness" with her, enriching our recipe book with dishes such as *pignatello saraceno* (mussel soup) on Fridays, *ragù con gli ziti* (long hollow pasta with a meat and tomato sauce) every Sunday, and so on.

The second Nonna Assunta

By chance, our paternal grandmother, who lived a little over five miles (eight kilometers) from Mamma Rosetta's house, was also called Assunta. This used to be a very common name, because it was connected with the Feast of the Assumption of the Blessed Virgin Mary (15 August), called Ferragosto in Italy, which is one of our biggest holidays.

The procession of Santa Maria Valogno

On that day in Santa Maria Valogno, near Sessa Aurunca, the village where the Nonna Assunta on our father's side was born, there is a large procession and a big fireworks display. At Ferragosto, they eat more than ever and the menu is set by tradition.

And the lunch...

The evening before Assumption day, the famous *ceci e taglierini* (chickpeas with taglierini, see page 73) was eaten. This was also offered to the members of the group of musicians who would follow the statue of Our Lady in the procession the following day. On the saint's day itself, there were ziti (long hollow pasta) with ragù (see page 83), the famous piece of stuffed meat stewed in tomato sauce for hours and hours.

Then there was roast kid, chicken, *insalata di rinforzo* (an appetizing bell pepper, olive, and anchovy salad, called *"di rinforzo"* because it is invigorating), *guanti* (deep-fried cakes that look a bit like gloves, see page 175), and so on. The preparations would begin at least a few days in advance.

Devotion

This festival was very important to our paternal Nonna Assunta because, among other things, she was very, very devoted to Our Lady—so much so that she once gave all her gold jewelry to the statue which was carried in the procession each year.

It seems that she did this because during World War II her eldest child Carmine (my father) had a miraculous escape from the machine guns of the SS. Basically, if anyone laid a finger on the Madonna, there was trouble. It goes without saying that everyone had to be there for lunch on Ferragosto.

Preparing for Assumption Day

Before there were any motor vehicles, Nonna Assunta and the other housewives used to get up at 3am to go and buy the meat for the ragù and the special Assumption Day *soffritto*—a breakfast dish made with lamb's offal, which strengthened the men before the hard work of carrying the statues of the saints in the procession. It had to be ordered a week beforehand from the butcher in Sessa Aurunca, which was over five miles (eight kilometers) away and a two- or three-hour walk. They would do anything to get the meat for the ragù: a piece of topside that was larded and stuffed with parsley and hard-cooked eggs.

Moral

As you will have realized, there was a lot of work behind a successful feast-day lunch. Usually the women would cook together as a group, because it wasn't worth working for days at a time for just a few people.

The whole family would gather together for the meal. So Nonna Assunta wasn't working by herself. Her sisters were there too, particularly Zia Flavia, who was so good at cooking that she gradually came to be known in the area as the person who cooked wedding buffets.

Wedding banquets

Ah, the weddings! Celebrating weddings in a restaurant is a relatively recent custom. At one time, wedding banquets were held at home. They were different from the lunches on saints' days. Endless cakes and cookies were baked for weddings, including various *taralli*, flavored with marsala or wild fennel seeds, fried cakes, and *freselle*.

To prepare all these good things required the help of women who specialized in baking this delicious food day after day. Zia Flavia was one of them. The wedding guests had to visit the bride's home a few days before the church service. "We took the big pieces of furniture out of the biggest room and put the chairs in a row," Rosetta tells us. "You sat there and the women went along the line with trays and glasses of liqueurs. It went on for quite a while. The guests would talk about the bride and groom, how and where they were going to live, the villagers, and life in general. Basically, anything that they were interested in. Sometimes people went on and on and they were even a bit of a bore if you were someone who preferred minding your own business." Well, Rosetta's never been that chatty.

The saints

Don't think that this is the end of the story as far as religious festivals are concerned! We're talking about villages in the south of Italy, where people are sincerely devoted to Our Lady and the saints. Not all of them, of course, but most are, and it's well known how important the saints are to Catholics.

So I really must tell you about the saint who, more than any other, enjoyed the devotion of Mamma Rosetta's family, as well as Rosetta herself. St Anthony of Padua is the Lato family's favourite saint, the most important, the best loved, and the one they think about most and whose name is most often spoken. Like St Gennaro for the Neapolitans, he is our patron saint.

St Anthony

This is a long story, woven into the life of generations of our family. For example, Nonna Assunta from Gaeta, Rosetta's mother, made a vow for my uncle, Zio Oristano, who was her eldest son. As a seventeen year old, having just passed his school-leaving exams, he decided to enrol as a volunteer and go to war. The Russian campaign has the unhappy reputation of having been one of the longest-lasting in World War II, with a very high casualty rate.

Well, Zio Oristano was in Russia and stayed there for five years, until 1946. For the last years of his time on the front, there was silence and no news came through at all. So Nonna Assunta made a vow to St Anthony that if Oristano came home she would wear the Franciscan habit for five years. He returned. Alone. Out of all the men from the area who had left with him, he was the only survivor.

The biggest party of all

I'm not sure just how soon the family organized a party to celebrate Zio Oristano's return, but they did. It was a real celebration with a brass band playing on the terrace. The adults and the elderly filled the inside of the house, while the young people danced on the terrace outside.

There were endless cakes, even more than at a wedding, and people came from other villages. Perhaps the only person who found that party confusing and embarrassing was Zio Oristano himself, whose stories about his time as a prisoner entertained us children throughout our childhood and after.

The vow

Not only did Nonna Assunta wear the habit for five years, but for the rest of her life she made a pilgrimage to Padua, to the Basilica of St Anthony, once a year, together with Nonno Antonio. On their return from one of these journeys, they brought home a statue of St Anthony over 3 feet (almost 1 meter) high, which was given a home on a table in the entrance hall of the house where Zia Idea, Rosetta's sister, lives now.

The statue is still there. That is where it belongs and no one would dream of moving it. Even in the 1984 earthquake, when a major tremor struck the house, leaving cracks which can still be seen in the walls, and all the things in the hall—vases, pictures, and everything—fell to the ground, not even the earthquake dreamt of moving that statue one inch. It was the only thing left standing in a sea of confusion.

More about feasts

I don't need to say that a week before 13 June, which is St Anthony's day, and was also Nonno Antonio's name day, there was already a festive air in the household.

The women would begin preparing the ingredients for the cakes, baking cookies, and starching tablecloths. Altogether, there was a great deal to do. Also, given that there were always a few guests eating at Nonno Antonio's table, just think what it was like on his name day! Sometimes there were even 35 or 40 people at the table.

Friends and relations came from the surrounding villages, who then returned the hospitality when it was their village's patron saint's day. Joining forces in the kitchen took on a fundamental importance, to say the least.

The women and the recipe book

This recipe book was created by these women, who together cover a period from the beginning of the twentieth century up to the present day. It is a century of stories and recipes, because a recipe book is enriched in this way, gathering ideas and suggestions from aunts, neighbors, friends, and acquaintances.

Since the women named above are only the tip of the iceberg, it can be said that they represent all the women whose creativity is expressed in the kitchen, daily repeating a sacred rite that is still very close to our hearts in Italy.

The author

I was born among these women and through a strange twist of fate I have found myself experiencing two particular aspects of life with particular intensity. I am a busy modern woman and, at the same time, I am a southern Italian woman who cooks because I am passionate about it.

My awareness of how quickly everything is changing has inspired me to make this recipe book available to everyone. I feel that it would be a real pity to let this inheritance be lost.

The places

Between vines, olive trees, and sweet chestnuts

Since Dionysus drank at just such tables made ready for feasting, you can well understand that this is not a story like all the others. In this case, nature has been particularly generous. The villages that play a key role in our stories are just a few miles away from one another: San Clemente di Galluccio, Sipicciano, Roccamonfina, San Carlo, Vigne, Cescheto, San Martino, Santa Maria Valogno, and Sessa Aurunca are all in a hilly area planted with vines and olives. These villages are linked by winding roads, which follow the line of the hillside.

The olive leaves are like a silver mantle spreading lazily down toward the plains and the sea in the distance, where Minturno and the gulf of Gaeta can be seen. In the other direction. the silver leaves go on up the mountain, becoming greener where the trees change from olives to chestnuts.

The houses

The old houses were built simply from large blocks of stone. Each house, however basic it may have been, had a wood-fired bread oven, which was built outside in the yard or sheltered by a small hut made of bricks.

The oven

The oven was very important. It was used for baking bread, which was made for the whole family at least once a week. It was wheat bread with an intense flavor, and stayed fresh for seven days or more. After baking the bread, the women would go on to roast meat and cook fish dishes, such as *alici arrecanate* (anchovies with oil, garlic, and oregano), and all the things that were usually prepared on the fire in the kitchen or on a small wood stove called a *fornacella*.*

We also shouldn't forget the pizzas with tomatoes, which are absolutely wonderful when they have the charred smell of burned wood. Dishes cooked on a wood fire have a different flavor—they are better. The oven was usually close to the kitchen, which was one of the most sacred places in the home. Almost everything happened there, and it was often the place where family life and social life came together.

The kitchen

People were happy to spend every moment of the day in the kitchen. My cousin Camillo, for example, was unable to settle anywhere else in the house without immediately feeling a strong longing for that spacious room, which according to the time of day took on a different light and atmosphere, and different smells.

In the morning, when lunch was being cooked, it was busy and chaotic. In the afternoon, during the siesta, it was silent and welcoming, becoming a place where people were not supposed to go, but into which they sneaked in order to steal a little of their favorite dishes that had been left to one side for the evening meal, or to take some cookies or chocolate. There was no end to the eating, tasting, and snacking.

Then came the time of day for coffee and visits. Elderly aunts, neighbors, and acquaintances dropped by to have a chat with Zia Carmela, bringing with them new-laid hens' eggs. These were good for making *uovo sbattuto*—egg yolk and sugar beaten with a teaspoon until it became thick and creamy like a custard. Or they brought a "finger" of homemade sausage, fresh salad greens, chickens, cakes, and whatever else was worth sharing with those who were dear to them. In the south of Italy, giving food is a sign of affection. The more special and difficult to find the gift is, the greater the love. What gift could possibly be more precious than something wholesome that often, of course, can't be bought in the stores?

So most of the family's time was spent in the kitchen, because cooking daily meals was only one of the many culinary activities that were carried out there.

*fornacella: this was a small wood-burning stove, which looked like a low masonry box. On the flat top were iron grills on which the pans were placed, and on the sides were small doors giving access to the inside of the stove, through which the fire under the grills could be fed.

WHY WERE THEY ALWAYS IN THE KITCHEN?

The thousand activities hiding behind a good meal

How does Mamma Rosetta cope with being in the kitchen all the time? It seems impossible, doesn't it? But that's how it is. For example, when I asked her to help me decipher and interpret the recipe book she had given me, not only did I decide to spend a month in her company, I also had to make quite an effort to get her attention.

I actually had to make appointments with her, and even that wasn't always possible. It was in the summer and it's well known that there's a lot to be done in the kitchen then. First the tomatoes needed to be bottled, which was quite a task, then there were the fruit juices, the peaches in syrup, the eggplants in oil, the *limoncello* liqueur, the homemade pasta because the next day a guest was coming or it was going to be a Sunday, and so on and so on. All this wasn't up to her. The ingredients dictated what had to be done, which meant that the work couldn't be delayed. For example, it takes hundreds of kilos of tomatoes to make enough passata, which we call *conserve di pomodoro*, to see our entire family through the winter.

These are bought from the market, but only when the right quality is available at the right price. As soon as the right San Marzano tomatoes, at the exact stage of ripeness needed, have been found, dozens of boxes are purchased. Shopping at the market is one of Papino's (Daddy's) jobs, and when he finds the produce he's looking for, he certainly doesn't hang around asking himself whether there'll be enough time to process it. In this way, we find ourselves with huge quantities of tomatoes or peaches or whatever at home, so then we have to get on with the job. If it is left around too long, the produce becomes overripe and then has to be thrown away, which would be an unacceptable waste.

It wasn't easy for me, contaminated as I am by the rhythms of modern life, to make a box of tomatoes or peaches my number one priority. On the other hand, the fact that it was necessary to behave like this wasn't even called into question. I've already said that for us to think of it as special, food has to be homemade, using really high-quality ingredients. This is particularly the case for the basics—so the oil, wine, passata, preserves, flour, fruit juices, jellies, and everything else have to be pure and unadulterated. If anything is missing, other family members or well-supplied friends are asked to help out. We swap things.

For instance, Zio Elio, Papino's brother who lives in the country, makes his own wine and olive oil, so our family gets all our wine and oil from him. Cooking a meal is thus only the last stage in a long series of preparations, the tip of the iceberg of traditional cookery. That is why I have decided to begin the many recipes in this book with a chapter about preparing basic ingredients, such as bottled fruit and vegetables, pasta, bread, and pastry.

The tomato...

It's well known that the introduction of the tomato to Europe was an almost revolutionary action. It was the Neapolitans, though, who fell head over heels in love with this fruit, since it was they who first discovered its hidden virtues as a food. Much has already been written about the romantic encounter between tomatoes and basil on a pizza and the magic that happened when tomato sauce was first paired with a plate of macaroni.

Like most indispensible items, tomatoes took their time to catch on. They arrived in Italy after the discovery of America, but it took another two centuries before what was thought of as just the fruit of an ornamental plant finally came to be appreciated for its delicious flavor and versatility in the kitchen. At first, it was thought the golden-red fruit of this beautiful plant (the reason for its Italian name *"pomodoro"*) were useful as an aphrodisiac, but when an eighteenth-century Neapolitan nobleman was hit over the head with a skillet while trying to seduce his serving-maid, tomatoes lost their kudos as a way of propitiating Eros and gained their current reputation as an irreplaceable ingredient in the kitchen.

This story reveals a great deal about the passionate character of Neapolitans, even though it may not actually be true. The poor gentleman resorted to the presumed aphrodisiac qualities of the tomato in an attempt to overcome his servant's resistance to his advances. He took three of the fruits and crushed them into the *soffritto*—the chopped onions and garlic—that she was frying in olive oil. Then he waited for her to try it, completely confident that this winning move would ensure him a night of burning passion. She, however, rejected his advances by hitting him with the skillet and then ran away. Disappointed and surprised, he consoled himself by eating what was left of the *soffritto* with the added tomatoes. That is when the love affair started. It was true love, the sort that is never forgotten, for a beloved that is greatly missed whenever it isn't there.

The nobleman was bowled over by the flavor of this delicacy and ordered that the red fruit be used for cooking from then on. It wasn't long before tomato sauce replaced the bell pepper preserve which until that time had been used in a similar way, and became the unchallenged queen of the Neapolitan table. It went well with pasta, fish, meat, eggs, vegetables, and other foods.

...and the passata

In short, nobody could manage without that red sauce any more. That's why they made an effort to find a way to make it available all the time—even in winter when there aren't any tomatoes—and came up with the idea of making passata. The ripe San Marzano tomatoes used to make it are on sale in the market in the first half of August.

Until a few years ago, when people still didn't have the necessary equipment to make passata on a large scale, a sort of tomato preserve was made using the strong summer sunshine. After crushing and salting the tomatoes, housewives poured the resulting sauce into several earthenware plates and protected them with a piece of cloth, then put them up on the roof or on top of a wall under the blazing sun, stirring them with a wooden spoon from time to time during the day. As the water evaporated from the sauce, it became more and more concentrated, and after several days, once it had grown very dense and dark in color, they poured it into a container with some of the tomato's inseparable partner, basil. They then poured a layer of extra virgin olive oil onto the surface. In this way, the preserved tomato sauce could be used right through the winter, diluted with a little water.

The opening of the first tomato juice factories had little influence on the peasant culture of farmers, who still prepare passata at home in a ritual that involves the whole family. Among my childhood memories is one of a major party lasting two or three days, to which everyone was invited. It wasn't enough to make just one sort of bottled tomato, the liquid passata; there were also the jars of tomato pieces, which were the hardest work. All of us children were called on to help with this stage of the work—the more of us, the better. We had to insert the long slices of San Marzano plum tomatoes, one by one, into the bottles. I'll leave the chaos created by a group of children busy doing such a job to your imagination. What's more, drips of juice ran down our arms from the tomato slices and burned our delicate skin, so after a few hours we ran out of energy and curiosity—still long enough for us to fill a good number of bottles. By then, the methods used for making passata had moved on a bit since the time of plates on rooftops, and the production chain was restricted to adults. There was someone putting the tomatoes through a special food mill, someone putting basil leaves into the bottles, someone pouring tomato juice into the bottles through a funnel, someone putting the lids onto the bottles, and someone putting them into the big iron cauldron, "*o caoraro,*" where they were boiled.

Since this is a ritual that cannot be abandoned, Mamma Rosetta still performs this difficult operation today, unperturbed and helped by Papino. I couldn't say which of them considers it more important to have bottles of their own homemade passata, but in any case it isn't questioned—they have to have their bottles. They also make them for their children and grandchildren. As well as the passata and the bottled tomato pieces, some of our family have recently started bottling peeled plum tomatoes.

Pomodori pelati
Peeled tomatoes

You will need some good firm plum tomatoes, such as the San Marzano variety, and clean, dry, hermetically sealed glass jars, such as Kilner jars. As usual, you will also need some basil leaves, which have been washed and dried. Bring a pan of water to a boil. Wash the tomatoes and scald them in the boiling water a few at a time, then remove them from the water and peel them very gently before they cool, taking care not to break them up.

Put the tomatoes in the jars, adding a couple of basil leaves to each jar. When each jar is full, put its lid on and place it in the pan, following the sterilizing directions given below.

How to seal the jars or bottles

If you're not using jars, it's best to use the sort of bottles that are used for beer, which can be closed quickly and easily with a crown cap using the appropriate gadget. Screw-top bottles are even quicker. If your bottles are the sort used for spumante, you'll need to use corks, which have been sterilized beforehand by boiling. The corks must be tied on well with string and the string then crossed over the cork and the top of the bottle. This takes some practice because if it isn't done properly there is a risk that the contents of the whole bottle could be ruined. Before putting the bottles or jars into a pan to be boiled, it is a good idea to turn them upside down for a few seconds to make sure that no liquid escapes.

Sterilizing

Once you have put the caps or lids on all the bottles or jars, place them in a very large pan with straw or pieces of cloth on the bottom of it so they don't break when the water is boiling. Pour on enough water to cover them, taking care to spread more pieces of cloth over the top of the bottles.

Cover the pan with a lid and bring the water to a boil. Boil peeled tomatoes and passata for 40 minutes and jars of tomato pieces for about an hour because they, unlike the others, are raw. Let the water cool before removing the bottles. Store them in a cool place. When this is done on a large scale, it usually has to be done outside on a wood fire or a large Calor gas ring.

Passata

Only people who live somewhere sunny like southern Italy and have plenty of time on their hands have the luxury of using the sun to make their tomato preserves. Another option is to make ready-to-use liquid passata and sterilize it by boiling the sealed bottles before it is stored in the pantry.

You will need plenty of ripe San Marzano plum tomatoes and some basil leaves. Wash the tomatoes and put a few of them at a time into a pan that is about a quarter full of water. When the water comes to a boil, the tomatoes will rise to the surface. Let them soften a little in the boiling water for a couple of minutes. Drain them in a colander and put them through a vegetable mill. This should give a fairly runny juice.

Wash some bottles thoroughly and let them drain. It's best to use bottles with a crown cap for this—see the recipe for *pomodori pelati* above. Using a ladle and funnel, fill the bottles, then add a few basil leaves to each bottle. Seal the bottles carefully, checking that they do not leak, then place them in a very large pan with pieces of cloth to protect them from breaking and boil them for about 40 minutes, as described in the recipe for *pomodori pelati*.

Homemade pasta

Until 50 years ago, people ate homemade pasta every day and didn't think of it as a specialty for major occasions. On feast days, everyone expected to eat *maccaroni*—that is, pasta made in a factory, which was also known as *pasta compra*, or store-bought pasta. Making pasta at home cost less, particularly if it was made using only flour and water, and since people tended not to be short of time, it was altogether natural to eat fresh pasta.

Nowadays, it's the other way round. People have plenty of money but not much time. So now factory-made pasta is our everyday food and fresh pasta has become something special. Of course, if you don't have time, you can buy fresh pasta in specialty stores, which sell all sorts of filled pasta as well as the simpler tagliatelle, pappardelle, and tagliolini. For those who want to have a go at their own handmade pasta, here's how to knead and work pasta dough. Good luck!

You will need a rolling pin and pastry board, a serrated or smooth pastry cutter, and a spatula for removing the dough from the pastry board. The pasta dough can be used in many ways: cut it into long thin strips for tagliatelle, or into very fine strips for tagliolini, which are also used in broth. For cannelloni and lasagna, on the other hand, the dough is cut into 3½ x 6in (8 x 15cm) squares, while for ravioli and agnolotti little 2 x 2in (5 x 5cm) squares are made, which are then filled and folded into various shapes

Quantities for the dough

1 egg and ⅔ cup (3½oz, 100g) flour are needed per person, so for 4 people:

> 2⅔ *cups (13oz, 400g) type "0" pasta flour*
> *4 eggs*
> *a pinch of salt*
> *1 tbsp extra virgin olive oil*

Heap the flour in a mound on the pastry board and make a well in the middle. Crack the eggs into the well and add the salt and olive oil, then start mixing the ingredients with a fork or wooden spoon, moving it downward from the top of the heap of flour and collecting a little of the surrounding flour each time. Take care to keep the outer circle of flour solid enough to prevent the eggs escaping while they are still too liquid.

The dough will gradually become firmer as the flour is worked into the mixture. When it is firm enough, start kneading it by hand and continue for 10–15 minutes, flouring the board every so often. Use a spatula to clean off any dough that sticks to the board and put it to one side. Knead the dough energetically until it is soft and well mixed. Every so often, stretch the dough out, then fold it back on itself, and start kneading it again. For a perfect result, it is important to knead the dough for enough time. When little bubbles start to appear in the dough, collect it into a ball, then sprinkle it with a little flour and let rest on the floured board for around 15 minutes, covered with a dish or a piece of cloth.

Rolling out the pasta

Cut the ball of dough into four pieces, each of which must be rolled out separately into a thin layer. This can be done using either a machine or a rolling pin. It takes a lot of skill and experience to roll pasta by hand, because you have to be careful to create a thin layer of dough without breaking it.

This is how to do it: take a piece of the dough and shape it into a ball with your hands, then flatten it a little with the palm of your hand and start rolling it with a lot of pressure on the rolling pin. It's good to start from the middle, giving the dough a quarter turn each time, which is important to keep its round shape and uniform thickness.

When the rolled-out dough begins to spread out, you will need to wrap it around the rolling pin and unroll it back onto the board after you have turned it, in order to avoid breaking it. The thickness of dough suitable for most purposes is around ⅛in (2mm). When you have rolled the dough to the desired thickness, let it rest for at least 15 minutes, then cut it as required.

Types of pasta

Tagliatelle: strips of pasta about ½in (1cm) wide. To make them, fold the rolled-out dough onto itself to form a fairly tight roll. Then, using a well-sharpened knife with a wide blade (if the knife is blunt, there is a risk of squashing the pasta rather than cutting it cleanly), cut the roll of pasta into ½in (1cm) strips. Next open out the rolls of pasta using your hands and the point of the knife, lifting them up and letting the tagliatelle fall loosely on to the board.

Fettuccine: strips of pasta about ¼in (5mm) wide. The method is the same as for tagliatelle. Tagliolini or taglierini are even narrower strips of pasta, around ⅛in (2–3mm) wide, again made in the same way. These are usually eaten in broth, but they are also good served as *pasta asciutta*, with a sauce.

Pappardelle: very wide strips of pasta, around 1in (2–2.5cm) wide. These are very good with a game and mushroom sauce, and also in a broth with pulses. Pappardelle can be made by cutting the rolled-out pasta directly, without rolling it, using a serrated pastry cutter.

Lasagna and cannelloni: wide strips of pasta, about 3½ x 6in (8 x 15cm) cut with a knife or a serrated pastry cutter.

Ravioli, agnolotti, etc.: pasta squares used for filled pastas of varying size, according to taste. The standard size is 2 x 2in (5 x 5cm).

Colored pasta

By adding green vegetables, carrots, beet, or even unsweetened cocoa to the normal dough, a great variety of colored pastas can be made.

La pasta verde
Green pasta

This is made by adding spinach to the dough. The quantities for 4 people are:

7oz (200g) raw spinach	*3 eggs*
2⅔ cups (13oz, 400g) type "0" pasta flour	*salt*

Wash the spinach and cook it in a pan with a pinch of salt but no extra water for 5–10 minutes. Let it cool, then squeeze the water out in a strainer and pass the spinach through a vegetable mill. When you place the flour on the pastry board, making a well in the middle, place the spinach in the middle together with the eggs and a pinch of salt.

  Then continue according to the method given for making and rolling the pasta dough (see pages 27–29). The quantity of flour may vary a little if the spinach has not had all the water squeezed out of it. It should also be remembered that the dough is bound to be thicker than that for plain pasta and it will tend to break more easily, as well as taking longer to dry.

Another way of making green pasta
You can use 7oz (200g) of tender young nettles instead of the spinach. The pasta will be particularly soft and tasty.

La pasta rossa
Red pasta

This is made by adding carrot purée and a little tomato concentrate to the dough. The quantities for 4 people are:

8oz (250g) carrots	*3 eggs*
1 tsp tomato concentrate	*salt*
2⅔ cups (13oz, 400g) type "0" pasta flour	

Wash and slice the carrots, then boil them in salted water until tender and put them through a vegetable mill. Cook the carrot purée in a pan with the tomato concentrate, stirring with a wooden spoon, until most of the water has evaporated, which will take 5 minutes.

  Remove it from the heat and let cool. Continue as for normal pasta (see pages 27–29). Put the flour on the pastry board, making a well in the middle, then place the carrot purée in the middle with the eggs and a pinch of salt. The red color gives a beautiful effect, but the dough cannot be rolled out as thinly.

BREAD, PIZZAS, AND PIES

The wood-fired bread oven—an essential feature of every home

In the past, even the poorest families were never without a wood-fired bread oven. The oven was one of the most important parts of the home, without which there was no bread, pizza, or any of the other delicacies. The oven was usually lit once a week to bake all the bread that was needed for the next seven days.

When there was a feast day or a wedding, the ovens were lit several days running for roasting meat, baking cookies, and cooking all the extra treats planned for the occasion. Wheat bread, whether white or whole-grain, remained fresh for many days, so six or seven big *panielli* were made at a time, saving the work of kneading and baking every day. *Panielli* were loaves of bread that were almost always round with a diameter of about 20in (50cm), which meant that they were big enough for even the largest families, who used to get through one of them each day. When the bread was ready, they went on to pizzas, as well as using the hot oven to cook other dishes or vegetables. They couldn't cook too many of these in advance because people didn't have refrigerators, so food had to be stored in the cellar, but they baked enough to make sure that each baking day was a bit of a party for everyone—or very nearly, anyway.

Before World War II, knowing how to make bread and get the fire in the oven ready, knowing the exact moment to put the bread into the oven and so on were all part of the store of knowledge and skills that a woman brought with her when she married. People thought that it wouldn't be easy for a woman who didn't know how to bake bread to find a husband. With this in mind, Nonno Antonio expected the teenage Rosetta to get up at 3am to mix and knead the bread dough by hand. He didn't make her do this because the family needed it, but so that she would learn for when she married. Of course, she wasn't very enthusiastic about this, but she didn't risk disobeying. So Zia Carmela and Mamma Rosetta reluctantly left their beds in the middle of the night to prepare the dough that would later be turned into pizzas, *focaccias, calzones,* and *panielli.* The morning after, they breakfasted on freshly baked bread, surrounded by an intense smell of tomato or vegetable pizzas.

On feast days, on the other hand, as well as baking bread and pizzas, they really went to town, making all the traditional foods that were served only once a year for that special occasion. At Christmas, the bread oven was used to cook all the traditional cakes (see *Desserts, cakes, and cookies*), as well as roast kid and chicken. At Easter, they baked sweet tarts with a rice filling and many different sorts of bread with particular shapes and fillings. These included ring-shaped loaves with eggs in their shells half buried in them—which fascinated small children—little "bread people" with hands and feet made of dough and coffee beans for eyes, and "*tortano imbottito*" (known as a *casatiello* in Naples), a ring of bread filled with salami and various cheeses and hard-cooked eggs. It isn't difficult to make, so a lot of people still cook it at home in their electric ovens.

The recipe I'm including here was given to me by Renato, a Neapolitan who cooks professionally because he's passionate about it—"*di professione per passione,*" as he himself likes to emphasize. Since he has a weak spot for *casatiello,* he has written a great recipe which, he assures me, "never fails to work." The recipes for the various tomato, vegetable, and mushroom pizzas, on the other hand, come from Mamma Rosetta.

Hand-made pizza dough

The pizza which has now become so well-known all around the world isn't at all difficult to make at home, even if you don't have a wood-fired bread oven. Here is the recipe for the base, to be used with whichever of the suggested toppings you prefer.

To make 4 pizzas

4 cups (1¼lb, 600g) type "0" pasta flour, plus
  extra for dusting
2 cakes (1½oz, 40g) compressed yeast

4 tbsp lukewarm water
4 tbsp extra virgin olive oil
2 pinches of salt

Dissolve the yeast in the lukewarm water. Put generous ⅓ cup (2½oz, 60g) of the flour on the pastry board, making a well in the middle, then place the dissolved yeast in the well. Mix carefully until the yeast is worked into the flour. Place the dough in a floured bowl and make a cross on its surface with the point of a knife, then let rise for around an hour in a warm place.

Then make a well in the rest of the flour and place the risen dough, oil, and salt in it. Knead together for about 10 minutes, adding a little tepid water at a time, until the dough is soft and velvety. Now let the dough rise for a few hours, letting it stand in a warm place in a mixing bowl (I use a soup tureen), covered with a cloth. When it has doubled in size, punch it down and work it again for a few minutes, then divide it into four.

Form each of the four pieces into a ball, then roll it into a nice round pizza shape, giving it seven quarter-turns as you work. Place the disks on the base of a well-oiled baking pan, then tap them with your fingertips to flatten them, so that the outside edges are a little thicker than the rest. Add your preferred topping (see the directions on the following pages).

Bake in the oven at 475°F (250°C) for a good 20 minutes. To be certain that it is well cooked, it's a good idea to check the bottom of the pizza, because the cooking time varies depending on the thickness and the type of topping.

Pizza dough made with a food processor

Mamma Rosetta wouldn't make her pizza dough with a food processor, but this is a useful recipe for busy people.

To make 4 pizzas

3⅓ cakes (2oz, 50g) compressed yeast	*4 tbsp extra virgin olive oil*
1 cup lukewarm water	*2 pinches of salt*
1lb 6oz (700g) type "0" pasta flour	

Dissolve the yeast in the warm water. Place all the ingredients in a food processor and process until the dough is soft and smooth. Collect the dough into a ball and cover it with a cloth, then let rise in a warm place for 3 hours.

Knock down the risen dough with your hands, then divide it into four. Form one of the four parts into a ball and roll it out on a floured work surface, giving it seven quarter turns until you have a nice round disk, 9in (22cm) in diameter. Place the disks on the base of a well-oiled baking pan, then tap the circles of dough with your fingertips to flatten them, so that the outside edges are a little thicker than the rest. Add your preferred topping (see the directions below).

Bake in a very hot oven, 475°F (250°C) for a good 20 minutes. To be certain that it is well cooked, it's a good idea to check the bottom of the pizza, because the cooking time varies depending on the thickness and the type of topping.

Pizza con pomodoro e acciughe
Tomato and anchovy pizza

Topping for each pizza

8oz (250g) fresh or canned peeled tomatoes	*a sprinkling of oregano*
2 tbsp extra virgin olive oil	*salt and pepper*
6 or 7 anchovy fillets	

Prepare the pizza dough according to the directions above and let rise. Once the dough has doubled in size, knock it down and knead it for a few minutes, then place it on an oiled baking pan, spreading it out until it's about ¼in (5mm) thick and tapping it with your fingertips so that you leave little dents in the dough.

Peel the tomatoes. Cut them into pieces and discard the pulp and seeds, then spread them over the pizza. Sprinkle the pizza with the oil, then break the anchovies into pieces and put them on top. Sprinkle on the oregano and add salt and pepper to taste. Bake at 475°F (250°C) for around 20 minutes.

Pizza con salsiccia e friarielli

Pizza with sausage and cime di rapa

F riarielli is the Neapolitan word for *cime di rapa* ("sprouting turnip tops," see page 57) which are used in a great many sauces and also on pizza, with their ideal companion, the sausage.

Topping for each pizza

10oz (300g) cime di rapa
1 sausage—about 5oz (150g); use an Italian
   sausage if available, or any good-quality pork
   sausages

2 tbsp extra virgin olive oil
1 clove of garlic, crushed
1 chile, deseeded and finely chopped
salt

Discard the stems and largest leaves of the *cime di rapa*, which will be too tough. Separate the florets and cut the more tender leaves into pieces. Wash the florets and tender leaves in plenty of cold water, then drain them. Prick the sausage with a fork. Fry the garlic, chile, and sausage in the olive oil and then add the *cime di rapa*. Add salt and cook on a low heat, stirring frequently, for about 45 minutes. Prepare the pizza dough according to the directions on page 32 (or page 35 if using a food processor) and let rise.

Once the dough has doubled in size, knock it down and knead it for a few minutes, then place it on an oiled baking pan, spreading it out until it's about ¼in (5mm) thick and tapping it with your fingertips so that you leave little dents in the dough. Bake in the oven at 475°F (250°C) for 20 minutes. As soon as the pizza is ready, cover it with the sausage and vegetables and serve while still hot.

Pizza e "menesta"

Pizza and greens

Menesta is a local word for green vegetables, particularly *scarole* (bitter curly endives), *cime di rapa* (sprouting turnip tops), broccoli, spinach, and Swiss chard. Unlike most pizzas, this one has a second layer of dough above the vegetables. It isn't difficult to make, and as it's very convenient for carrying about, it's ideal for picnics.

Serves 6

2 cakes (1¼oz, 30g) compressed yeast

1 cup lukewarm water

1¼lb (600g) type "0" pasta flour

4lb (2kg) green vegetables, such as
   endives or Swiss chard

5 garlic cloves

chile to taste

10 black olives, pitted and cut into pieces

10 green olives, pitted and cut into pieces

¼ cup olive oil

5 canned anchovies

salt

Dissolve the yeast in the water in a mixing bowl, then add a pinch of salt, the oil, and some of the flour. Start working the ingredients together with your hands, gradually adding a little flour at a time whenever the dough sticks to your hands too much. Knead the dough until it is soft and velvety, remembering that the more you knead it, the better the pizza will be. Cover it with a cotton cloth and then a woollen one and let rise for a few hours in a warm place.

While the dough is rising, wash the green vegetables and parboil them for 3 minutes in a very small quantity of salted boiling water. Drain them, then squeeze out any remaining moisture and chop them. Fry the garlic cloves, chile, and olives in the oil in a skillet for 5 minutes, then add the vegetables and anchovies. Mix it all together and cook until any liquid has evaporated.

Once the dough has doubled in size, knock it down and knead it for a few minutes, then divide into two, one a little larger than the other. Place the larger piece on an oiled baking pan, spreading it out until it is about ¼in (5mm) thick and tapping it with your fingertips so that you leave little dents in the dough. Next spread the filling evenly over the dough, then roll out the other piece of dough and place it on top. Crimp the edges with your hands so the two halves are well attached to one another and bake in the oven at 475°F (250°C) for about 30 minutes. To make sure that it is cooked, check that the bottom of the pizza is golden-brown.

Pizza fritta
Fried pizza

Pizza dough can also be used to make this typical Neapolitan specialty, which is rather like a *calzone* filled with fresh tomatoes, mozzarella, and basil, but instead of being baked, it is fried. My mother wouldn't dream of frying in anything other than Zio Elio's cold-pressed extra virgin olive oil; sunflower-seed oil will work perfectly well, though.

For each pizza

5oz (150g) fresh tomatoes

5oz (150g) cubed mozzarella cheese

2 basil leaves, torn

1 tbsp extra virgin olive oil

salt and pepper

oil for frying

Prepare the pizza dough according to the directions on page 32 (or page 35 if using a food processor) and let rise. Once the dough has doubled in size, knock it down and knead it for a few minutes, then roll it out to a thickness of about ¼in (5mm). Prepare the filling by peeling the tomatoes and removing the pulp and seeds inside, then cut them into small pieces and mix them with the cubed mozzarella, torn basil leaves, and salt and pepper, and sprinkle with the olive oil.

Place the filling in the middle of the pizza, then fold it over into a half-moon shape as if it were a *calzone*. Close the edge carefully with a knife blade and your fingers. Fill a skillet three-quarters full of oil (with the oil about 1 in/2.5cm deep), then heat it until it is very hot and then fry the pizza. Cook the pizza until it is golden, then drain it on absorbent paper towels. Serve immediately.

Calzone

A *calzone* is a pizza that has been filled and folded over, like a half-moon. The filling can vary depending on your taste and imagination. The ingredients suggested below are the ones that are traditionally used to fill *calzoni* in Naples.

For each calzone

2oz (50g) mozzarella cheese

3½oz (100g) salami

basil

½ cup grated Parmesan cheese

¼ cup ricotta cheese

1 egg yolk for glazing

salt and pepper

Prepare the pizza dough according to the method on page 32 (or page 35) and let rise. Once the dough has doubled in size, knock it down and knead it for a few minutes, then place it on an oiled baking pan, spreading it out until it is about ¼in (5mm) thick.

Cut the mozzarella and salami into cubes and tear the basil into pieces, then mix them with the Parmesan, ricotta, salt, and pepper.

Place this mixture in the middle of the disk of dough, then fold it in half, closing the edge carefully by pressing on it with the point of a knife and your fingers. Paint the surface with the beaten egg yolk. Bake in the oven for 15 minutes at 400°F (200°C), then turn the heat down to 340°F (170°C) and cook for an additional 15 minutes.

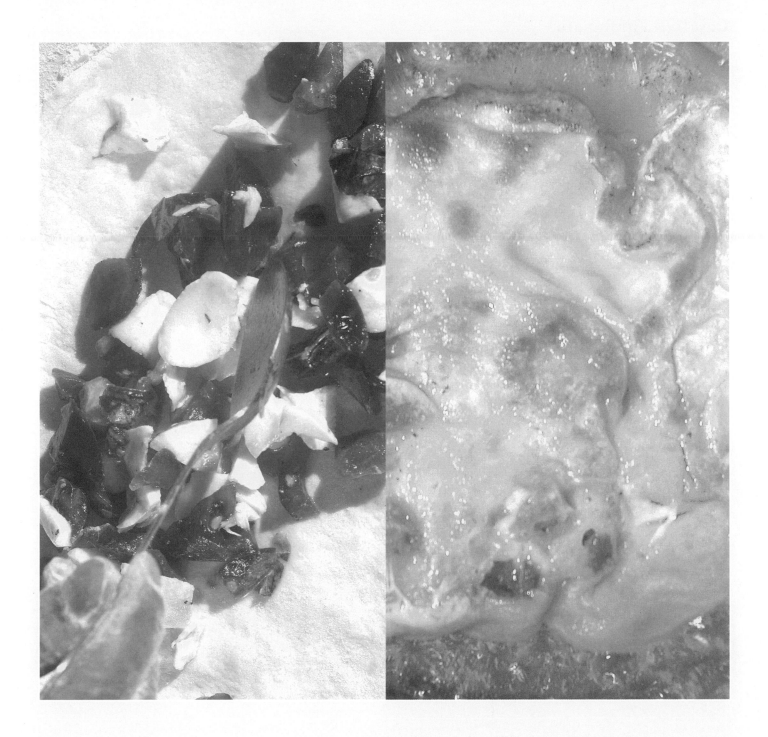

Casatiello di Renato
Renato's casatiello

The original recipe for *casatiello*, a savory pie that is usually cooked at Easter time, also includes hard-cooked eggs in the filling. However Renato, who is a great *casatiello* expert, prefers to serve the hard-cooked eggs separately, as a side dish, along with a salad. In his opinion, hard-cooked eggs would stop the bread around them cooking properly, leaving it a little too moist. Perhaps this specialized refinement is the secret that makes this pie so good.

For the dough

  1½lb (750g) type "0" pasta flour
  2½ cakes (1½oz, 40g) compressed yeast
  ¼ cup lukewarm water
  3 tbsp lard (or shortening)
  3 tbsp extra virgin olive oil
  salt and pepper

For the filling

  12oz (350g) salami, cubed
  12oz (350g) mild cheese, such as
    Gruyère, cubed
  freshly ground black pepper

Place the flour on a pastry board, making a well in the middle. Dissolve the yeast in the warm water, then add salt and pepper and pour into the center of the flour. Mix and knead it all together, then let rise for about an hour. Once the dough has doubled in size, work the lard into it by tearing off pieces of dough, wrapping each one over a piece of lard and then reincorporating them into the mixture. Doing this will ensure that, once it is cooked, the dough will be as crumbly and light as shortbread.

Roll the dough out to a thickness of ½in (1cm) and fill it with the pieces of Gruyère, salami, and a sprinkling of pepper. Now form the dough into a roll, joining the two ends to make a ring. Place it on a well-oiled baking pan and place in a preheated oven at 400°F (200°C). Bake for 30 minutes with the pan on the base of the oven, in direct contact with the source of heat, and for 30 minutes at the center of the oven—so for 1 hour in all. It is better not to use a pan that is too thin and light, to avoid the risk of burning the *casatiello*.

Pane di mamma Rossella
Mamma Rossella's bread

This is a quick recipe, which is handy if you want to have a go at baking bread at home. Mamma Rossella, who passed the recipe on to Mamma Rosetta, often uses it, more because she enjoys kneading than because she really needs to.

Ingredients

¾oz (20g) active dry yeast
generous 2 cups lukewarm water
a pinch of salt
1 tsp sugar

¼ cup olive oil
about 2lb (1kg) type "0" pasta flour
a handful of pitted olives (optional)
a handful of shelled walnuts (optional)

In a large mixing bowl, dissolve the yeast in about ¼ cup of the lukewarm water and add the salt, sugar, and oil. Gradually add more water and the flour, kneading it energetically, then add the olives and nuts (if you're using them—it's also good without them) and knead for about 10 more minutes.

Form the dough into a round loaf and place it on a greased pan. Cover it with a cotton cloth and then a woollen one, and let rise in a warm place for a few hours. Bake in the oven for 1 hour at 400°F (200°C).

HUGE HOMEMADE BUFFETS

How could anyone forget the *taralli* and *crespelle*, the heart of any home-cooked banquet—never missing from the buffets of wedding receptions held at a family home? Until about 50 years ago, people in my family's neighborhood didn't celebrate weddings in restaurants, because the custom was to organize very elaborate homemade buffets. It took at least three or four women to prepare the food. They spent day after day doing nothing but baking cookies and *taralli*.

When Papino and Mamma Rosetta got married, 42 years ago, there were three women in Don Antonio's house who spent an entire fortnight taking one exquisite delicacy after another out of the wood-fired bread oven. What's more, theirs was a double wedding. Rosetta was married at the same time as her sister, Idea Vittoria, who married Carlantonio Di Stasio from San Carlo, a village about four miles (six kilometers) from San Clemente. It was the first time that a double wedding had been celebrated in San Clemente, so a great many people visited the home of the two brides in the days before it. All of them brought gifts and they were all welcomed into the room that had been decorated for the reception. The guests were offered *crespelle*, which are fried savory rings of bread that are also made for New Year's Eve, and *taralli*, sweet ones, ones made with lard and pepper, and the two sorts made with fennel seeds—twisted ones made without yeast, and smooth ones made with it.

Next came the *guanti*, which were never lacking from the buffet table at a party (see page 173). *Guanti* are big fritters tied in a loose knot to make a shape that looks a bit like a glove; they are always served on any major occasion. Then came the sweet *freselle*, excellent cookies that can also be used for everyday breakfasts, and *pan di spagna* with *crema pasticcera* (see page 170). All this was eaten with dessert wines and liqueurs. These were the delicacies that guests could expect to taste in the bride's home, and they were rarely disappointed—everyone did their best for a wedding banquet.

Crespelle

Crespelle are ring-shaped donuts, made using a dough that is similar to the one used for bread, and fried in olive oil. They were always made for New Year's Eve, too.

Serves 4

1 tbsp olive oil
1¼ cakes (¾oz, 20g) compressed yeast
1¾ cups lukewarm water

2⅔ cups (13oz, 400g) type "0" pasta flour
1 tbsp salt
olive or sunflower-seed oil, for deep-frying

Grease the inside of a large bowl, such as a salad bowl, with a tablespoonful of oil. Dissolve the yeast in about ¼ cup of the lukewarm water, then add the rest of the water and the flour and salt. Mix with your hands, working the dough up the sides of the bowl as you knead it. Knead the dough in this way for at least 15 minutes until it is evenly mixed and not too dense. Let rise in a warm place for about an hour.

Heat olive or sunflower-seed oil to a depth of about 1in (2.5cm) in a skillet over moderate heat. When the oil is very hot, tear off fist-size pieces of dough and shape them into a ring, then place them in the boiling oil, using the handle of a wooden spoon to help you to keep the hole in the middle open. Fry the *crespelle*, turning them so that they are golden-brown on both sides, then remove them from the oil and let drain on absorbent paper towels. They are best served hot.

Taralli col finocchietto attorcigliati

Twisted taralli with fennel seeds

These *taralli* are made without yeast. They are boiled in salted water and then baked. Each time we make *taralli* we make a lot of them, because they keep well for a month. These quantities can, however, be halved, if preferred: you will get fewer *taralli*, but you'll spend less time in the kitchen baking them.

2lb (1kg) type "0" pasta flour	*4 tsp salt*
¾ cup extra virgin olive oil	*3 tsp fennel seeds*
generous 1½ cups water	

Mix all the ingredients in a large bowl, such as a salad bowl, until they are evenly mixed. If the dough is too sticky, add more flour until it separates easily from the bowl's sides.

Since this recipe contains no yeast, it doesn't need a lot of kneading. Tear off small pieces of dough and form them into little sticks, about ¼in (5mm) wide and 16in (40cm) long. Bend each stick of dough back on itself so that you get two sticks, each of them about 8in (20cm) long, then twist them together and join the ends to make a double twisted ring. Bring a pan of salted water to a boil and place four or five *taralli* in the water at a time. Use a spoon to stop them sticking to the bottom of the pan and wait until they rise to the surface by themselves.

When they have come to the top, remove them from the water using a slotted spoon and place them on a clean dish towel to dry. Next arrange them on a baking pan, without oiling it (*taralli* already contain enough oil to stop them sticking), and bake them in the oven at 350°F (180°C) for about 20 minutes, turning them over after about 10 minutes. Remove them from the oven when they are golden brown and set them aside. Continue in this way until you have finished all the dough.

Taralli con il lievito

Yeasted taralli

1⅔ cakes (1oz, 25g) compressed yeast	*2 tsp fennel seeds*
1¾ cups lukewarm water	*1½ tsp salt*
generous ¾ cup extra virgin olive oil	*2lb (1kg) type "0" pasta flour*

Dissolve the yeast in a little of the lukewarm water, then add the rest of the water and the oil, fennel seeds and salt and mix with the flour. Knead until you have a smooth, soft dough. Let rise in a warm place for a few hours until it has doubled in size (the time depends on how warm it is: the warmer the place, the less time it takes).

Tear off little pieces of dough and form them into sticks as wide as your thumb and about 8in (20cm) long. Join their ends to form them into rings and place them on an unoiled baking sheet. Bake in the oven at 350°F (180°C) for about 20 minutes.

FRUIT AND VEGETABLE PRESERVES

It's always very satisfying to find that you have a few jars of artichokes preserved in oil in the pantry, or some really good jelly that you've made yourself or have been given by somebody. I've noticed for some time how welcome the gift of a jar of homemade passata, jelly, or a few bottles of homemade fruit juice can be.

The old belief among farming people, that nothing is more welcome than the gift of some wholesome produce which not even money can buy, is still up to date, and not only in farming communities. Mamma Rosetta knows all about this, and this is why she continues undaunted with her ancient ritual of making preserves.

In the past, bottling fruit and vegetables was a necessity, both because it was impossible to buy these products out of season and because there was sometimes a glut of them, making it impossible to use them all and meaning some would have to be thrown away. These days, preserves are made because it's traditional and just because they taste nice. The recipes given here are the ones that meet two essential needs nowadays: they are simple and taste good.

Carciofini sott'olio
Artichokes preserved in oil

2lb (1kg) tender young artichokes (If you are buying them in Italy, ask for primaticci or marzaioli)
2 lemons, sliced
generous 2 cups white wine vinegar
generous 2 cups dry white wine
a handful of salt

3 garlic cloves, sliced
1 tbsp chopped parsley
1 tsp black peppercorns
a small piece of fresh red chile
extra virgin olive oil

It is best to use artichokes that are very young and tender and freshly harvested. Remove the toughest leaves and thorns, leaving ½in (1cm) of stem, and place them in a bowl of water, with slices of lemon added to prevent discoloration. Meanwhile, bring the vinegar, wine, and salt to a boil. Add the artichokes and cook them for 3 minutes, stirring them with a wooden spoon. Drain them and arrange them head down on a piece of cloth to dry for 12 hours.

Take one or more hermetically sealable jars (such as Kilner jars) and place the artichokes in them in layers, alternating them with garlic, parsley, peppercorns, and chile. When the jar is full, cover it all with extra virgin olive oil. Using a slotted spoon to keep the artichokes well squashed down, so they don't rise above the oil, seal the jars and store them in a cool, dark place. It is best to wait at least 30 days before eating them.

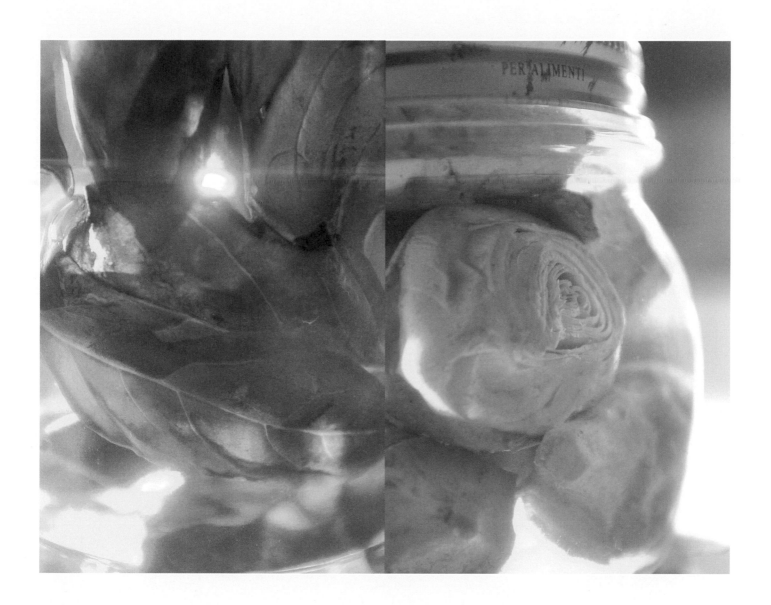

Peperoni sott'aceto
Bell peppers preserved in oil

These are the bell peppers used to make salads, together with boiled potatoes and other vegetables. They are also excellent with chicken cooked with olives, oregano, and capers, or fried with oil, a few garlic cloves, a handful of bread crumbs, and a sprinkling of vinegar.

2lb (1kg) bell peppers (weight after preparation) *1 tbsp sugar*
1 tbsp fine salt *½ cup wine vinegar*

Obtain bell peppers when they are in season (in July or August), and wash and dry them. Deseed them and cut them into pieces, narrow strips, squares—or in half if you want to use them for stuffing—whatever you prefer. Their weight after you have prepared them must be exactly 2lb (1kg). Place them in a glass salad bowl, adding the salt, sugar, and vinegar. Mix well and let marinate for 5–6 hours, stirring frequently so that all the peppers are exposed to the liquid equally.

Take one or more glass jars (such as Kilner jars) and fill them with the bell peppers. Add the liquid, making sure that it comes right to the top of each jar, covering them completely. Any bell peppers that are not covered will become too soft. Seal the jars and place them on a piece of cloth in the bottom of a pan. Cover the jars with another piece of cloth, then fill the pan with water and heat it on the stove. Wait until the water comes to a boil and then time it for exactly 5 minutes. Then take the jars out of the water and let them cool. Store in a dry, dark place.

Before using the bell peppers in any dish, rinse them under running water in a colander. Remember that when you open the jar the bell peppers at the top will be a little soft. You can throw them away and use the ones below, which will have the right, slightly crunchy consistency.

Olio al basilico
Oil with basil

This is a nice easy way to store basil and to create a flavored olive oil. It is an ideal seasoning for *insalata caprese*, a salad made with slices of tomato, mozzarella, basil, and a pinch of oregano.

about 30 basil leaves *generous 2 cups extra virgin olive oil*

Wash and dry the basil leaves and place them in a 17fl oz (500ml) bottle. Fill the bottle with olive oil, seal it hermetically with a crown cork (or similar; see the recipe for passata, page 25) and boil in a large pan of water for 30 minutes. Remove the bottle from the pan and let cool. The oil will keep in the storecupboard for at least a year.

Jellies

M amma Rosetta sterilizes her jellies by boiling them after she has put them into the jars. She maintains that this ensures that the jellies keep for a long time without any problems.

Marmellata di mele alle rose
Apple and rose preserve

4lb (2kg) sweet-smelling, full-flavored apples
grated zest and juice of 1 lemon
1lb (500g) scented fresh rose petals

1 cup water
3lb (1.4kg) sugar

Peel the apples and cut them into pieces, then place them in a large non-aluminum pan with the grated zest and juice of the lemon. Wash the rose petals in cold water, then drain them and add them to the apples.

Mix thoroughly and add the water, then cover and let rest for a half-hour. Place the pan on low heat and bring to a gentle boil, stirring and skimming off any foam. When the apples are cooked, pass it all through a hair strainer (which is what we use, but a nylon strainer will do), then return the purée to the pan. Add the sugar and bring slowly back to a boil, stirring frequently. As soon as the mixture has begun to thicken a little, but while it is still fairly liquid, remove it from the heat and ladle it, while it is still hot, into hermetically sealable glass jars (such as Kilner jars) that have been preheated in a bain marie or a warm oven.

When pouring the hot preserve, take care not to place the jars on a cold surface, or you may break them. Leaving about ½in (1cm) between the preserve and the top of each jar, seal them and let cool. Place a clean cotton cloth on the base of a pan, then put the jars on top. Fill the pan with warm water, then cover it with a lid and bring the water to a boil. Boil for 40 minutes, then turn the heat off and let cool. Take the jars out of the pan and put them into the pantry.

Marmellata di fichi
Fig jelly

2lb (1kg) figs
juice of 2 lemons

1 cup (7 oz, 200g) sugar

Peel the figs and break them into small pieces, then add the lemon juice and sugar and place it all in a non-aluminum pan. Cook over moderate heat, stirring frequently with a wooden spoon. Boil until the jelly is ready. To check whether the jelly has been cooked enough, pour a little onto a small plate and tip it to one side. When the jelly runs down the plate very slowly, it is ready.

Pour the jelly into hermetically sealable glass jars (such as Kilner jars) which you have preheated in a bain marie or a warm oven. When pouring the hot jelly, take care not to place the jars on a cold surface, or they may break. Leaving about ½in (1cm) between the jelly and the top of each jar, seal them and let cool. Place a clean cotton cloth on the base of a pan, then put the jars on top. Fill the pan with warm water, then cover it with a lid and bring the water to a boil over low heat. Boil for 40 minutes, then turn the heat off and let cool. Take the jars out of the pan and put them into the pantry.

Pesche sciroppate
Peaches in syrup

generous 2 cups water
1 cup (7oz, 200g) sugar

4lb (2kg) yellow peaches (I use the
 "Gialloni" variety)
juice of 2 lemons

Pour the water into a pan, then add the sugar and place on the heat. Stir constantly until the sugar has dissolved, then bring to a boil and boil for 5 minutes. Remove the syrup from the heat and let cool.

Peel the peaches and cut them into ⅜in (7–8mm) slices. Put them in a salad bowl and sprinkle them with the lemon juice to prevent discoloration. Place the peach slices into hermetically sealable jars (such as Kilner jars), then pour the cold syrup over them and seal the jars hermetically. Place a clean cotton cloth on the base of a pan, then put the jars on top. Fill the pan with cold water and cover it with a lid, then ring to a boil and boil for exactly 4 minutes. Turn off the heat and remove the jars from the pan immediately so that the peaches stop cooking. Let cool and store in the pantry.

ANTIPASTI

Antipasti have never been an essential part of the cooking tradition of the area that produced the recipes in this book—at least, not as far as everyday meals were concerned. At most, the family sometimes decided to serve an antipasto on feast days. On the evening of Christmas Eve, for example, which is when we had our main Christmas meal, we traditionally started with a dish of *cime di rapa*, which was stewed and then sautéed with garlic and chiles.

For our New Year's Eve dinner, on the other hand, we had fried *crespelle* (see page 45) and also *mazzabuotti*, which were the main dish. *Mazzabuotti* are made with a mixture similar to bread dough and shaped like rissoles, with pieces of stewed salt cod, cauliflower, anchovy, or fruit hidden inside them. They are served in enormous baskets, so it's very difficult to see from the outside what is hidden inside them. It's a matter of luck whether you fish out your preferred fritter or not, so everyone at the table often jokes about that and has a good laugh.

At Easter, hard-cooked eggs reigned supreme among the antipasti, halved and sprinkled with olive oil and salt. They were arranged on a plate with sliced salami, *capocollo* (cured pork), spicy smoked sausage, *ricotta salata*, and anchovies. The star of our interminable feast-day meals was, however, a salad with a bizarre name: *insalata di rinforzo* (invigorating salad), which could never be missing from the menu for a special occasion at home. On such a day, my grandfather wouldn't even have sat down at the table without his *insalata di rinforzo*. It simply had to be there. This salad was eaten as an antipasto, as a side dish, and as an appetizer between courses. It made its appearance on the table at the start of the meal and stayed there until the time came for the dessert to be brought, when it was moved to the kitchen, where it was left for anyone who still wasn't quite full to have a bit more. It's called "*di rinforzo*" because, with the bell peppers and vinegar that are its main ingredients, it whets the appetite and aids digestion. It's helpful at those critical moments when you've already eaten a lot but you want to carry on, because the meal isn't over and delicious food is still arriving on the table.

Stuffed chile peppers also enjoy a reputation for whetting the appetite and aiding digestion and are sometimes served as an antipasto. A real delicacy, they aren't at all difficult to prepare. In this chapter, I have given the recipes for some of the dishes mentioned above, together with other little treats which have been added to our family recipe book over the years. In the chapter on vegetables, you will find more dishes that can also be used as antipasti.

Insalata di rinforzo

Bell pepper, olive, and anchovy salad

We make this in large quantities. If any is left over, it keeps well in the refrigerator.

6 large bell peppers of any color: red, yellow,
  green and/or orange
1 garlic clove, chopped
25 green olives
white or red wine vinegar, to taste

10 fillets of salted or canned anchovies in oil,
  cut into pieces
extra virgin olive oil
salt

Wash the bell peppers and parboil them in water for 1 minute. Drain them and cut them into long thin strips. Place them in a salad bowl and sprinkle them with wine vinegar (it doesn't matter whether it's red or white). Let the bell peppers rest for a few hours while they take on the flavor of the vinegar.

Taste the bell peppers, adjusting the quantity of vinegar to get the flavor and intensity you prefer. If you find them too sharp, drain off the vinegar and rinse them a little. Next add the olives, garlic, and anchovies, then dress with olive oil and season with salt.

Peperoncini tondi ripieni

Stuffed round chiles

12 round chiles
½ cup water
½ cup red wine vinegar
4oz (100g) tuna

1 tbsp anchovy paste
12 capers (optional)
extra virgin olive oil

Remove the seeds from the chiles. Bring the water and vinegar to a boil and scald the chiles in it for 1 minute, then drain them. Mix the tuna and anchovy paste together and use the mixture to stuff the chiles. If you like, you can also place a caper inside each chile.

Arrange the stuffed chiles in a glass jar and cover them with oil. Let them stand for a few days, then serve as an antipasto or a snack.

Mazzabuotti di fine anno
New Year mazzabuotti

The dough used for *crespelle* can also be used to make *mazzabuotti*, which are fairly large fritters with pieces of salt cod, cauliflower, anchovies, or fruit inside them. Obviously you can vary these ingredients according to your taste and what is available. They are all brought to the table together on one plate, so it is very difficult to tell what the filling is from the outside.

Serves 4

For the dough

2 cakes compressed yeast
2½ cups lukewarm water
1¼lb (600g) type "0" pasta flour
2 tsp salt
olive or sunflower-seed oil, for deep-frying

For the filling

3½oz (100g) salt cod, soaked in water
   for 48 hours
10 canned anchovy fillets
3½oz (100g) cauliflower florets
2 apples

Mix the yeast and a little of the lukewarm water in a bowl, then add the rest of the water. Sift the flour and salt together and add them to the bowl a spoonful at a time. Mix the flour, salt, and water with your hands to make a dough, working it up the sides of the bowl as you knead it. The dough should be rather soft and sticky and slightly stringy. Leave it to rise in a warm place for at least half an hour.

Meanwhile, drain and wash the salt cod and check it carefully for bones. Wash the cauliflower florets, then salt them and place them on absorbent paper towels for a good 10 minutes until they are dry. Cut all the filling ingredients into regular ¾in (2cm) square pieces. Dip them into the risen dough one at a time and deep-fry them in oil which is boiling, but not yet smoking. You will need to fry the *mazzabuotti* in plenty of oil to ensure that they absorb as little as possible. Place them on absorbent paper towels to drain, then heap them in a pyramid on a serving dish.

Antipasto di Pasqua: uova sode e soppresse

Easter antizo: hard-cooked eggs and charcuterie

Soppressata is a sort of cured pork, which comes from the area around Naples. Pork is cured in slightly different ways all over Italy to make charcuterie such as *coppa di Parma, lonza,* or *capocollo.*

   Always home-cured, using various parts of the pig that each family has been fattening up all year, a southern Italian *soppressata* has an intense flavor, which is difficult to describe. Served with hard-cooked eggs, it is the traditional antipasto for Easter Day. As the years have gone by and people have become wealthier, housewives have added salami, sausage, and raw, dry-cured ham to this dish.

Serves 6

6 hard-cooked eggs
6 slices of soppressata
6 slices of spicy smoked sausage
6 slices of ricotta salata cheese (hard salted ricotta)

6 anchovies
extra virgin olive oil
salt

Cut the hard-cooked eggs in four lengthwise. Arrange the pieces of egg in a circle on a round or oval plate, placing a slice of *soppressa* between each piece of hard-cooked egg, and so on with the other ingredients. Sprinkle with olive oil and season with salt, then serve.

Insalata di mare

Seafood salad

Serves 6

1lb 10oz (800g) mussels
1¼lb (600g) clams
3 garlic cloves, cut in half
⅔ cup extra virgin olive oil
1¼lb (600g) shrimp

1¼lb (600g) small squid
1 bunch of parsley, chopped
juice of 1 lemon
salt and pepper
1 tsp mustard (optional)

Wash the mussels and clams. Now sauté a garlic clove in a pan with few spoonfuls of olive oil and add the shellfish to the pan. When they have opened, shell them and put them in a salad bowl. Strain the cooking liquid and use it to boil the shrimp for 4 minutes. Add these to the mussels and clams, again reserving the cooking liquid.

   Clean the small squid, then cut them into rings and boil them in the same cooking water that was used for the shrimp for 4–5 minutes. Drain them and add them to the salad bowl. Dress them with chopped parsley and the remaining garlic, the lemon juice, salt, pepper, and the rest of the oil. If you like, you can also add a teaspoon of mustard. Mix it all together and let rest for a few hours before serving. Let stand in a cool place, but preferably not in the refrigerator.

Scapece

S capece is a marinade based on vinegar and natural flavorings, which has been used since ancient times to preserve fish and vegetables for long periods. It seems that its name is derived from the recipes of the Roman cook Apicius, who was unequalled for his concoctions of vegetables and sauces based on macerated fish guts.

Caelius Apicius, who lived in the time of Tiberius (1st century AD), was a true celebrity. He left us *De re coquinaria*, a 10-volume treatise on cooking, which includes the first description of a liquamen based on mint, garlic,and white wine vinegar, in which fried fish and vegetables were marinated. At that time it was called *esca Apici*, "Apicius's sauce," which the Neapolitans later corrupted to "*a scapece*."

Tradition has it that Lucullus employed Apicius as his cook and took him along when he moved to *Castrum Lucullianum* (his splendid Neapolitan villa) to cook his famously lavish feasts. *Scapece* is found throughout southern Italy and, as well as being used with anchovies, it is also excellent with eggplants, sliced zucchini, and pieces of large zucchini and fish that have been floured and then fried. The vinegar it contains it makes it an excellent appetizer. I have given two versions here, the first with mint and the second with oregano.

Melanzane alla scapece (con la menta)
Eggplants in scapece (with mint)

2lb (1kg) eggplants
olive or sunflower-seed oil, for frying
*   the eggplants*
2 garlic cloves, crushed
¼ cup extra virgin olive oil, for the marinade

1 bunch of mint
1 red chile, deseeded and chopped
3 tbsp white wine vinegar

Peel and slice the eggplants and fry them in plenty of olive or sunflower-seed oil. Leave them on absorbent paper towels for about 10 minutes to drain away excess oil, then place them in a soup tureen. Now fry the garlic in the extra virgin olive oil for a few minutes until transparent. Remove it from the heat and add the mint leaves and chile.

Return the pan to the heat and after about a minute add the vinegar and let reduce. Pour the liquid onto the eggplants and let marinate for at least half a day.

Alici alla scapece (con l'origano)
Anchovies in scapece (with oregano)

Serves 4

2lb (1kg) small fresh anchovies
2 cups (10oz, 300g) semolina flour
olive or sunflower-seed oil, for frying
generous ¾ cup wine vinegar

4 garlic cloves, finely chopped
a pinch of oregano
salt
pepper or chili powder, to taste

Wash the anchovies, then remove their heads and fillet them. Next, coat them with the semolina flour. Heat the oil in a pan until boiling and fry the anchovies for about 3 minutes until crisp and golden on the outside.

Transfer the anchovies to a soup tureen. Boil the vinegar for a few minutes with about 1 tablespoon of water, then add the finely chopped garlic, oregano, salt, and pepper or chili powder. Pour the hot liquid over the anchovies and let marinate for at least a day.

Spiedini di mozzarella con melanzane
Mozzarella and eggplant kabobs

Serves 4

10 tomatoes
1 tbsp oregano, chopped
3 eggplants
10oz (300g) mozzarella cheese
3 x ½in (1cm) slices of good-quality white bread

olive or sunflower-seed oil, for frying
plain flour, for coating
3 eggs
salt and pepper

Wash and dry the tomatoes, then slice them and season them with the oregano. Cut the eggplants and mozzarella into approximately ¾in (2cm) cubes. Heat some oil in a skillet and fry the eggplant cubes, then transfer them to absorbent paper towels. Cut the bread into cubes. Thread a bread cube, a piece of mozzarella, a slice of tomato, and a cube of eggplant alternately onto each of 8 skewers.

Sprinkle some flour onto a plate. Crack the eggs into a bowl and beat them lightly with a pinch of salt and pepper. Dip each kabob into the flour and then into the beaten eggs. While you are doing this, heat more oil in a skillet. Once the oil is hot, fry the kabobs until they are crisp and golden.

Insalata quattro stagioni
Four seasons salad

This salad is excellent in summer, as an antipasto for lunch or the evening meal, or served by itself as a light lunch.

Serves 6

4 potatoes
3 eggs
1 red bell pepper
3 tomatoes
8 scallions
10oz (300g) canned tuna in oil
3oz (80g) canned anchovy fillets in oil
10oz (300g) green beans, boiled and cut in pieces

5 pickled gherkins, sliced
scant 1¼ cups black or green olives, pitted
5 tbsp extra virgin olive oil
1 tbsp mustard
a squeeze of lemon juice
chopped herbs: thyme, marjoram, basil,
* and parsley*
salt and pepper

Wash and boil the potatoes, then let cool. Peel the potatoes and slice them, then place them in a salad bowl. Hard-cook the eggs, then cool them under running water. Shell the eggs and cut into fourths. Wash the bell pepper, then dry it and halve it. Remove the stem, seeds, and white pith and cut it into narrow strips. Wash, dry, and slice the tomatoes. Trim and wash the scallions. Add the strips of bell pepper, sliced tomatoes, and scallions to the bowl.

Break the tuna into pieces and add it to the bowl. Add the anchovies, green beans, sliced gherkins, and olives, then mix gently. Arrange the quartered hard-cooked eggs around the top of the salad. In a small bowl, beat together the olive oil, mustard, lemon juice, and salt and pepper. Pour this dressing over the salad and the eggs, then sprinkle it with the chopped herbs.

TRADITIONAL ONE-DISH MEALS

Perhaps these are some of the most ancient recipes in this book. Because they are very good and very simple, they have been passed on from generation to generation, unaffected by any type of outside influence. At one time, elaborate dishes such as game and other cooked meats, often cooked in the French manner, were to be found only at the courts of great lords. In Naples when the Bourbons were on the throne, the nobility made many attempts to supplant the local food tradition with French cuisine. I hardly need to tell you that this didn't work.

On the contrary, it was the French nobles and their supporters who had to give way to the strength and flavor of Neapolitan cooking. Indeed, it wasn't unusual for them to stop to eat simple but delicious food on the street or in the trattorias, food that was perhaps even better than what they ate at court. Among the dishes they enjoyed were *zuppa di soffritto*, a soup made of pork offal, *friarielli (cime di rapa)*, and of course macaroni, for which Neapolitans have become famous all over the world. In the countryside around Naples, peasant farmers and the common people ate vegetables and cereals. They rarely ate fish and on feast days they had meat.

In the area these recipes come from, the pasta dishes described here were eaten only on feast days. The pasta that was cooked in soups was made at home using only flour and water. Since they were very filling and nourishing, these soups were a meal in themselves. They were eaten with excellent homemade wheat bread, cooked in the wood-fired bread ovens that were found in even the poorest homes. The soup and bread were both dressed with olive oil and, in the best Mediterranean tradition, a glass of wine was drunk with the meal.

Minestrone

Serves 4

1 onion, chopped
6 tbsp olive oil
2 celery stalks, chopped
2 carrots, sliced
2 red tomatoes, chopped
1 cup water
piece of Parmesan or romano cheese rind,
   about 1 x 2 in (2.5 x 5cm)
7oz (200g) fresh peas, shelled
7oz (200g) green beans, cut into short pieces

7oz (200g) swiss chard, coarsely chopped
2 potatoes, cut into fairly small pieces
stock (optional)
2 zucchini, sliced
7oz (200g) fresh cannellini beans, already cooked
salt
chili powder
2 garlic cloves
5 basil leaves
4 tbsp grated Parmesan cheese

Sauté the onion in 5 tablespoons of olive oil in a large pan. When the onion has turned transparent, add the celery, carrots, tomatoes, water, and cheese rinds, then add the peas and green beans. After 5 minutes, add the chard and potatoes, then add enough hot water to half fill the pan, or stock if preferred. After another 5 minutes, add the zucchini and cook for an additional 5 minutes. Now add the cooked cannellini beans, then mix it all together and let the flavors blend for 5 minutes. Add salt to taste and a pinch of chili powder.

Use a pestle and mortar to make a pesto from the garlic, basil, and grated Parmesan. When they are ground to a paste, mix them with a little olive oil and add to the minestrone. Mix well and serve. This dish is excellent served hot or cold.

Fasuri, accio e pommarola

Fava beans, celery, and tomatoes

This recipe is best made in summer, when fresh fava beans, celery, and tomatoes are available. It can, however, be made in winter using dried beans instead of fresh and the celery that is now available all year round. The beans are traditionally cooked in a *pignato*—a tall, narrow, earthenware cooking-pot—which is placed near the heat, not directly over a flame. This type of pot is best used on a wood-burning stove or next to an open wood fire.

Serves 4

1lb (500g) fresh fava beans

fresh herbs: thyme, rosemary, sage, and bay leaves

1 head of celery, including the leaves—about

  1lb (500g)—finely chopped

1 onion, finely chopped

3 tbsp olive oil

1lb (500g) fresh tomatoes, cut into small pieces

a pinch of salt

Shell the beans and place them in a tall, narrow, earthenware pot (or large pan), then add the herbs and cover with water. Cover the pot and boil it next to (or on) a gentle heat for 1½ hours.

Fry the celery and onions in the oil in a large, low-sided, flameproof earthenware pan. Add the tomatoes in small pieces; you can liquidize them if you like, but be careful not to chop them too finely. Let the pan stand on low heat until the sauce has thickened.

When the beans are ready, pour them into the sauce with a little of the cooking water, then add the salt and let stand on moderate heat for 5–8 minutes.

Zuppa di soffritto
Offal soup

This is a typically strong and tasty winter soup, which was always on the menu at the old osterias. Ninuccio's osteria, in Via Santa Lucia in Sessa Aurunca, was famous as a destination for important people, who would stop there to eat this specialty made from red pork offal. When a portion was ordered, Signora Maria, the innkeeper, put a little of the soup in a pan with some bay leaves, which helped to tone down the flavor of the fat.

The soup is served poured over slices of bread or with pasta that has been drained while it is still *al dente*. It is still made in some osterias in Naples.

Serves 4

2lb (1kg) pork offal
1 oz (30g) lard
5 tbsp extra virgin olive oil
½ cup red wine
1 onion, chopped
2 bay leaves

1 sprig of rosemary
1 red chile, or more to taste
1lb (500g) passata
6 cups meat stock
salt and pepper

Wash the meat in cold running water, leaving it under a slowly running faucet for a few hours, then cut it all into small pieces. Fry it with the lard and 2 tablespoons of the olive oil. After a few minutes, add the red wine and let evaporate.

In a separate pan, sauté the chopped onion, bay leaves, rosemary, and chile (whole or chopped) in the remaining olive oil. Pour on the passata and season with salt and pepper. Simmer for 30 minutes over low heat, then push it through a strainer.

Mix the sauce with the offal and cook it for about an hour, still over low heat, adding a little stock from time to time. Once it is ready, the soup can be poured over bread crusts or eaten with the pasta of your choice.

Minestra di fave e cicoria
Fava bean and chicory soup

Chicory (*Chicorium intybus*) is much used both as a green vegetable and as an ingredient for soups. A bitter-tasting loose-leaved form of chicory, it grows just about everywhere in this area of Italy, even on roadside verges.

Legend has it that an unfaithful girl was changed into a chicory plant by a devil, who wanted to punish her for her infidelity. The roots and leaves of chicory are used in traditional medicine as a bitter tonic, a purifier, diuretic, and vermifuge, and for reducing a fever. As well as this, for many centuries its roots have been dried, roasted, and ground to be used as a coffee substitute.

The only problem is that wild chicory can be too bitter for some people. To overcome this, the chicory is rinsed quickly under cold water as soon as it is drained from the cooking water, but is still boiling hot. This reduces the bitterness and makes even the bitterest chicory good to eat.

Serves 4–6

6 cups shelled fresh fava beans
6 cups water
2 bunches chicory, about 1lb (500g)
2 onions, halved and sliced

4 tbsp extra virgin olive oil
1 small handful of basil leaves
salt

Boil the fava beans in the water. Drain them, reserving the cooking water, and pass half of them through a food mill. Wash the chicory and parboil it in the cooking water from the beans, then cut it into pieces

Sauté the onions in a skillet in 2 tablespoons of the oil for a few minutes, then add the chicory, the puréed beans, a little of the cooking water, and the remaining beans. Bring this to a boil, then remove the pan from the heat. Season with salt, then dress with the rest of the oil and garnish with the basil leaves.

Ceci e taglierini–'saette e tronole'

Chickpeas and taglierini–'thunder and lightning'

This is another very old recipe. It is said that in 1139 Pope Innocence II, who had lost in battle to King Roger II of Sicily, fled to Santa Maria Valogno, a small village near Sessa Aurunca, and knocked on a farmer's door, without saying who he was. Although he didn't recognize him, he gave him *ceci e taglierini* to eat and a place to sleep. At around the same time, the image of Our Lady of the Assumption was found in a myrtle grove.

Once the war was over and things had been sorted out with the Norman king, the Pope returned to Santa Maria Valogno, this time in his papal vestments. He granted indulgences and ordered a celebration and a great feast to be celebrated in the honor of Our Lady of the Assumption of the Myrtle Grove. He also ordered that chickpeas and taglierini be eaten on the eve of the feast day. Since then, on each 14 August, the musicians whose band is to accompany the statue of the Madonna in procession are invited to a meal by the families of the village. The first dish they are served is *ceci e taglierini* (chickpeas and pasta), which is also called "thunder and lightning" because of the well known wind-producing effects of the chickpeas.

Zia Flavia tells a story that when she was young, about sixty years ago, her family hosted two of these musicians—in this case, two trumpet players—who were left to sleep in a room where some beans had been left to dry. Those two poor musicians were so hungry that the next day they went away with the beans inside their trumpets, thinking that nobody would see.

Since this is a frugal dish, taglierini were made at home using just water and flour. If you don't have enough time to roll out the pasta dough, you can use store-bought tagliatelle.

Serves 4–6

10oz (300g) chickpeas
a pinch of salt or 1 tsp baking soda
8 tbsp extra virgin olive oil
2 garlic cloves, chopped
2 onions, chopped
a pinch of chili powder
1 bunch of herbs: sage, bay leaves, rosemary,
*   basil, and pennyroyal*

5 fresh tomatoes
3 basil leaves
8oz (250g) taglierini, made using 8oz (250g)
*   type "0" pasta flour according to the method*
*   on pages 27–29, but with as much water as*
*   you need instead of the eggs, or 8oz (250g)*
*   dry tagliatelle, broken into small pieces*

Soak the chickpeas overnight in warm water, adding a little salt or baking soda. Rinse them the day after and cook them in a *pignato*, a tall, narrow, earthenware cooking-pot (or a large pan) on or near a very slow fire, together with the garlic, onion, chili powder, bunch of herbs, 4 tablespoons of the olive oil, and enough cold water to cover them (otherwise the chickpeas will become hard). When the chickpeas are tender, drain them, reserving the cooking water, and set aside.

Fry the remaining onion in 4 tablespoons of oil. When it is soft, add the tomatoes and basil leaves to make a light, runny sauce. Cook for 15 minutes, then add the chickpeas with a little of the water they were cooked in and leave for another 15 minutes so the flavors can mix. When it is nearly ready, cook the pasta in salted boiling water. It is better to do this in a separate pan, because the pasta needs to be cooked in boiling water and the chickpeas can't be cooked over high heat. This also has the advantage that any flour stuck to the pasta won't end up in the soup.

As soon as the pasta has risen to the surface, remove it with a slotted spoon and add them to the soup. Mix carefully and serve straight away. This dish can be garnished with fresh basil.

Zuppa di cozze al pomodoro
Mussel and tomato soup

Serves 4

3 garlic cloves
4 tbsp extra virgin olive oil
10oz (300g) peeled plum tomatoes,
  coarsely chopped

2lb (1kg) mussels, well scrubbed and washed
1½ tbsp chopped parsley
pepper
4 slices of toast

Chop 2 of the garlic cloves and fry them in the olive oil, then add the chopped tomatoes. Once the sauce is ready—when the oil has separated from the tomatoes—add the mussels. Then add the parsley and pepper. The soup is ready as soon as all the mussels are open. Rub the toast with the remaining whole garlic clove and place a slice in each bowl. Pour the hot soup over the toast and serve.

Zuppa di lenticchie e cime di rapa
Lentil and turnip-top soup

Cime di rapa (sprouting turnip tops), also known as *broccoli di rapa* (but not to be confused with broccoli), are called *friarielli* in Naples and *broccoletti* in Rome. A real institution of Neapolitan and southern Italian cookery in general, they are quite delicious in soups, or stewed and then sautéed in olive oil with chiles.

    Neapolitan *friarielli* are said to be even tastier than the Roman ones, because they are grown on the fertile soil around Mount Vesuvius. Like other products from this area, which is rich in mineral salts, they are particularly good to eat.

Serves 4

To cook the lentils

13oz (400g) green or brown lentils, soaked in
  water for 12 hours
broth from the salami, as needed
2 bunches cime di rapa, about 1lb (500g)
1 garlic clove, chopped
4 tbsp olive oil
10oz (300g) mixed pasta—different shapes

For the broth

1 small cacciatore salami (a mildly seasoned
  coarse-cut, pure-pork salami)
1 onion, chopped
1 celery stalk, chopped
1 carrot, chopped
6 cups water
salt

Place the salami and all the other ingredients for the broth in a pan. Bring to a boil, then let simmer for about 5 minutes. Set aside about 1¼ cups of the broth, in case you need it to make the soup less thick later on. Wash the soaked lentils and boil them in the rest of the broth with the salami, adding salt to taste. Meanwhile, boil and drain the *cime di rapa*. Fry the garlic in the oil in a skillet, then add the *cime di rapa* and sauté them. Finally, add all this to the broth with the lentils. Bring to a boil and add the mixed pasta. The consistency of this soup is a matter of personal taste, so you can add more broth if you wish while the pasta is cooking, as long as the broth you add is already boiling.

Polenta con broccoli neri
Polenta with black broccoli

Just as in Naples people eat macaroni, in northern Italy polenta is the staple food. That's why southern Italians, whom northerners call *terroni*—an insulting term meaning "country people"—get their own back by calling the northerners *polentoni*, which means "polenta-eaters." For this reason, it's strange to find a recipe for polenta in a typically southern cookery book.

What's even stranger is that this dish of "green" polenta is eaten only in Ciociaria, in southern Lazio, in the area near Frosinone, Sora, and Cassino. Neither northern Italians nor Neapolitans are familiar with green polenta. Mamma Rosetta, on the other hand, cooks it almost every week in winter, just as naturally as she cooks other dishes that she has learned from Zia Carmela. San Clemente is actually much closer to Cassino, in Ciociaria, which is only about 20 miles (30 kilometers) away, than it is to Caserta, about 40 miles (65 kilometers) away, or Naples.

Of course, the food traditions of a farming area like Ciociaria have had a strong influence on the neighbouring area around San Clemente, which in its turn has also been influenced by Neapolitan cuisine.

Serves 6

2lb (1kg) broccoli neri (use purple sprouting broccoli, or try cime di rapa or curly kale)
6 cups boiling water
5 tbsp extra virgin olive oil
coarse sea salt

chili powder
1lb (500g) polenta (it's better to use the coarse-grained polenta bramata, rather than the instant sort)

To prepare the broccoli, break off the flowering heads and cut the small tender leaves into pieces, discarding the thick stems and any large leaves, which may be tough. Wash it in plenty of cold water and drain, then place in a pan containing the boiling water. Boil for 5 minutes, then add the oil, salt, and chili and turn off the heat.

Let rest for a few minutes, then turn the heat back on and start pouring in a thin stream of polenta, letting it fall in like rain, a little at a time, while stirring constantly with a wooden spoon so that no lumps are formed. Continue to stir with the wooden spoon, while leaving it to cook over moderate heat. The polenta is ready when it separates from the sides of the pan.

Serve straight away, or let cool and set for use the following day, when it can be cut into pieces and sautéed with a little olive oil.

Fagioli e scarola

Beans and bitter curly endives

You can also make this dish with *cime di rapa* instead of endives, which gives the soup a stronger flavor.

Serves 4

400g (13oz) *dried beans (white or red,*
   e.g. cannellini or cranberry), soaked
   in water for 12 hours
1 *small onion, chopped*
2 *garlic cloves, crushed*
1 *celery stalk, chopped*
1 *tbsp chopped parsley*

2oz (50g) *pancetta (optional)*
6 *tbsp olive oil*
1lb (500g) *scarola (bitter curly endives)*
   or cime di rapa
salt and chili powder
slices of toast

Drain and wash the beans and then boil them until tender; drain and reserve the cooking water. Using an earthenware pan if possible, sauté the onion, 1 of the garlic cloves, the celery, parsley, and, if you are using it, the pancetta in 4 tablespoons of the olive oil. Cook for about 10 minutes, then add the beans with a little of their cooking water and let the flavors blend together.

Meanwhile, wash the endives and boil them until they are *al dente*, then chop them coarsely. In a third pan, sauté the remaining garlic clove in the rest of the olive oil, then remove it. Add the boiled, chopped greens and let them cook together for a short while so the flavors blend, then add the greens to the beans, taking care that the mixture is not too dry or too watery. Season to taste with salt and chili powder and let rest for 10 minutes, then serve hot with toast.

PASTA

Most people don't realize this, but dried pasta—the sort that's sold everywhere in packages—has been around for a very long time. It seems to have been invented by Arab nomads, who discovered how convenient it was to take sun-dried pasta made from flour and water with them when they were traveling, instead of having to make it from scratch each time the caravan stopped for a meal. Given that the Arabs were already in Sicily in the 9th century, it was natural that this pasta, known as *maccaroni*—but which the Sicilians called *itrija* (the Arab term for vermicelli)—became the Sicilians' favorite dish and that making it developed into one of the island's main trades.

Sicily's hot sun lent itself very well to drying vermicelli. The artisan production of macaroni spread throughout southern Italy, but it was in Naples, and more precisely in Torre Annunziata, that pasta production on a truly industrial scale began. It was also thanks to the Neapolitans and the famous Pulcinella that macaroni gained in popularity, and was already well known outside Italy in the eighteenth century. Pulcinella's costume, with its jacket pockets stuffed full of steaming hot macaroni, became famous all over Europe. Because of this, the Neapolitans came to be known as "*maccaronari.*" At one time in Naples, macaroni was also cooked in the open air, at little mobile stalls.

There was one stall in particular, in Via Chiaia, which was renowned because the *maccaronaro* who ran it had a small oil painting with six lamps in front of the steaming cauldron of pasta. Next to it he placed the bowls of grated cheese, and then he surrounded the whole thing with a sea of flowers. The pasta was served in a paper cone, dressed with a little pork fat and a handful of romano cheese, and, later, with tomato sauce too.

Ordinary people ate it with their hands, as can be seen in the famous old film *Miseria e nobiltà* (*Poverty and nobility*), starring Totò, Italy's greatest comedian, in which he tosses handfuls of pasta into the air and tries to maneuver his open mouth into the right place to catch them as they fall. Further evidence of people's love of pasta comes from the area of Sessa Aurunca, where many years ago those in power would buy hundreds of kilos of packages of macaroni before the local government elections. The pasta was used literally to "buy" the votes of peasant farmers who were still uneducated and over-respectful to the *padrone* who owned the land and gave them work. One vote per package and the die was cast—everyone loved macaroni.

The name macaroni is commonly used to refer to long pasta of any sort, whether it has a hole through the middle or not. This ranges from zitoni, a sort of pasta with a big hole which can also be stuffed, to ziti (the macaroni of the *zita*, which is Neapolitan for "bride"), to bucatini, a sort of pasta with a very small hole, called *perciatelli* in Naples. Vermicelli, on the other hand, are a little thicker than spaghetti.

In my nonna's time, they cooked ziti on feast days. They were served with ragù and everyone adored them. My uncle Franco, who is just over 60 now, has told me that as far as he's concerned ziti are the best pasta in existence. He likes them served with a sauce made of spare ribs and tomatoes. Of course, each time I visit him he cooks this for me and I lick my lips. The long sticks of ziti have to be broken up because otherwise they would be too inconvenient to eat. Some people say they should be broken into three pieces, some into four.

This is not a negligible detail because it is precisely the ziti's irregularity that the Neapolitans like so much. Recently Zio Franco told me how difficult it is to get hold of ziti outside Naples. He lives in the north of Italy, and each time he goes out to buy some it's like mounting an expedition. Apparently only two of the pasta companies which distribute throughout Italy still make ziti, and this sort of pasta is probably even rarer abroad. Don't forget, though, that if you can't get hold of ziti, you can use rigatoni, penne, sedanini, or other sorts of short pasta tubes.

Ziti, ragù, and the feast day meal

Ragù

An irreplaceable feature of Sunday lunches, Neapolitan ragù contains within itself the essential qualities of the tomato, but also, and more specially, those of a people. There's nothing people in Naples wouldn't do for a good ragù! Many poets, singers, actors, and writers have extolled the virtues of this sauce. Quite simply, Sunday isn't Sunday for Neapolitans without it.

To be made well, ragù has to simmer (or, as we say in Naples, *pippiare*) for at least five hours, during which time it is forever being stirred, checked, and made a fuss of; it is never abandoned to its own devices. Ragù is something so personal that each neighborhood in Naples has its own way of making it. Some people make it with just a piece of beef, some put a bit of pork in as well, some include a carrot and celery, some add red wine and some white.

There are a great many variations, but at the end the essence of the sauce doesn't change very much and people still cook with the same passion. What's more, people in Naples say that a true ragù can be cooked only by someone who feels intense love for at least one of the people who will eat it.

Il ragù della festa di ferragosto

Here is the recipe that is used to make the ragù for the Ferragosto feast at Santa Maria Valogno, Nonna Assunta, and Zia Flavia's village. All the neighbouring villages also make it the same way.

Unlike in Naples, the women use hard-cooked eggs as part of the stuffing for the meat in the ragù. "We made a pesto out of parsley and *lardo,* or else cured ham, and put it into the meat, a long round piece," Zia Flavia told me. "We made a big hole in the middle and put a bit of pesto, a hard-cooked egg, a bit more pesto, and another egg into it, until we had filled right along the meat. When it was cut, the slices were round, with the egg in the middle. It tasted good, too, because it was cooked in an earthenware pot over a wood fire. It took the whole of the day before the feast to make the ragù.'

When the dish is brought to the table, the yellow egg yolks surrounded by the green of the pesto and the dark red of the *sugo* (tomato sauce) create an explosion of color. This is a dish that is made to be shared, and the eyes are the first to feast on it.

The feast-day lunch

As well as flavoring the *sugo* to eat with the dish of ziti, which reigns supreme over the first course, the meat from the ragù is served later as an entrée. To be precise, it's served as the second entrée, after the roast lamb with potatoes and before the roast chicken with salad.

All this is washed down with generous glasses of wine and accompanied by bell peppers, *melanzane alla parmigiana* (baked eggplants), and the inevitable *insalata di rinforzo* (see page 55), which is there to whet the appetite and aid digestion. It shouldn't be forgotten, either, that the men who worked their way through all this had already had a sizeable breakfast that same morning when the day was traditionally begun with the celebrated *soffritto.*

Zia Flavia told me that *soffritto* was expensive, so few people could afford it: "so it was only eaten on that feast day. On that occasion," continues Zia Flavia, "as well as the *soffritto,* we cooked chickens with rosemary, oil, and parsley, kid and all the vegetables. We cooked all of it in the bread oven, because we didn't have gas. Nobody went to bed the night before Ferragosto. They all stayed awake baking food, while Assunta and I went to buy the meat."

The feast-day meal continues with *guanti* (see page 175). More recently, we have started to serve cake and fruit salad. Last but not least came the coffee, with three Cs, as Nonna Assunta from Gaeta used to say, standing for *"come caspita coce,"* which means *"mamma mia,* how hot it is!" Only then, after coffee, at about five o'clock on a sunny August afternoon, when there's a relaxed holiday mood, can one leave the table to doze in the shade of a tree, savoring the warmth of the party that is over and enjoying the silence of the countryside, interrupted only by the song of the cicadas.

Feast-day ragù

Serves 8
For the meat

3½oz (100g) pancetta, in one piece
3½oz (100g) prosciutto or cured ham, in one piece
1 good-sized bunch of parsley, chopped
2lb (1kg) lean beef (at Carnival pork fillet
  is used)
4 hard-cooked eggs, shelled
pepper
1lb 5oz (650g) ziti and grated Parmesan cheese,
  to serve

For the sugo (tomato sauce)

¼ cup extra virgin olive oil
5oz (150g) lardo (salted pork back fat)
2 garlic cloves, chopped
15oz (450g) onions, chopped
1 celery stalk
3 small carrots, chopped
1 cup dry white wine
3 cups passata
8oz (250g) tomato concentrate, dissolved in
  about ¼ cup warm water or meat stock
1 tbsp chopped basil
a good pinch of nutmeg
salt and pepper

Cut the pancetta and prosciutto into narrow strips, then add the chopped parsley and a good pinch of pepper and mix it all together to make a pesto. Take the piece of beef and, using a knife with a long thin blade, made a hole right through the middle so it becomes a long tube: it's a good idea to ask your butcher to do this for you when you buy the meat. Next, insert the parsley pesto and hard-cooked eggs into the meat alternately, reserving some of the pesto. Close each end of the beef with kitchen thread and set the remaining parsley pesto aside.

Put the oil, *lardo*, chopped garlic, onions, celery stalk, and carrots in a pan over moderate heat. It's best to use an oval earthenware pan if you have a suitable one. Stir the mixture continually until the onions have softened a little. When they begin to brown, add the reserved parsley pesto and turn up the heat, then add the meat, turning it so that it browns evenly. Turn the heat down and add the white wine a little at a time, letting it evaporate while you carry on stirring with a wooden spoon, taking care that the ingredients do not burn.

Once a thick dark gravy has formed around the meat (this will take about 2 hours), add the passata and diluted tomato concentrate a little at a time. Stir it and simmer over very low heat, adding more tomato as needed. After another hour, add the basil, nutmeg, and salt and pepper and carry on cooking until the tomato is finished and the *sugo* turns a nice brownish color.

When you see that the meat is cooked, remove it and continue to let the *sugo* simmer. If it starts to get too dry, add hot stock or hot water (stock is better) little by little, until it is shiny and very dark in color.

Since ragù takes such a long time to cook (5 or 6 hours), it is a good idea to make it a day before it is needed. This way, you can also remove the excess fat that will be found on its surface the day after, if you want to. Slice the meat and serve it hot as an entrée. Cook the ziti in the same way as you would cook any pasta, but remember to break each stick into at least three or four pieces.

As well as eating the sauce from the ragù with ziti or other sorts of pasta, you can use it to make lasagna and cannelloni. Don't forget to sprinkle a little grated Parmesan or seasoned romano and some freshly ground pepper onto the pasta before you eat it.

Ziti alla maniera di Zia Carmela
Zia Carmela's ziti

Serves 6

13oz (400g) ground beef
2 garlic cloves, crushed
1 large onion, finely chopped
1 celery stalk, chopped
5 tbsp extra virgin olive oil
¼ cup dry white wine
2 cups peas (shelled)
13oz (400g) passata
a handful of fresh basil leaves, torn into pieces
a pinch of chili powder

oil, for frying the eggplants
2 eggplants
1lb (500g) ziti (or rigatoni, if you can't find ziti)
3 hard-cooked eggs
7oz (200g) provola cheese
3 tbsp grated romano cheese
1 tbsp chopped parsley
salt and pepper

Brown the meat, garlic, onion, and celery in a skillet with the oil. When the meat is well browned, add the white wine and let it evaporate. Then add the peas, passata, torn basil leaves, and chili powder. Season with salt and pepper and simmer over low heat for 1 hour.

Cut the eggplants lengthwise into thin slices and fry them in plenty of oil, then place them on absorbent paper towels and set them aside to drain. Cook the pasta in plenty of salted boiling water and drain it while it is still very *al dente*. Dress the pasta with the meat and pea *sugo*, hard-cooked eggs, provola, and romano, and sprinkle with the chopped parsley.

Place the slices of fried eggplant on the bottom and around the sides of a buttered ovenproof dish with sides at least 2in (5cm) high, then add the pasta and bake at 350°F (180°C) for 15 minutes, until the top is crispy and golden.

Fusilli, spaghetti, and more ...

Fusilli con uova e formaggio
Spirals with eggs and cheese

Serves 6

1 large onion, finely chopped
⅞ stick (3½oz, 100g) butter
1¼lb (600g) fusilli (pasta spirals)
5 eggs

½ cup (2oz, 50g) grated romano cheese
¾ cup (3½oz, 100g) grated Parmesan cheese
salt and pepper

Fry the onion in the butter in a skillet over low heat. Boil the pasta until it is *al dente*, then drain it and add it to the onion, keeping the heat very low. Beat the eggs and mix them with salt, pepper, and the grated cheeses, then stir them into the pasta and onion. Let the pasta stand to take on the flavor of the sauce for a few minutes, then serve.

Spaghetti olio, aglio, peperoncino e acciughe
Spaghetti with olive oil, garlic, chile, and anchovies

Those who know a bit about pasta know that this is the simplest dish of all, the one which is usually made at the last minute, when people are really hungry and nobody wants to wait even a minute more, or when you meet up with a group of friends in the middle of the night and you decide to eat a plate of spaghetti and nobody wants to waste any time making *sugo*.

Spaghetti with olive oil, garlic, and chile is the solution for even the worst-stocked pantry—all you need is some olive oil, some garlic, and a pinch of chilies—things which are normally always to be found in any Mediterranean kitchen. The variant with anchovies that I give here is excellent. For a long time, the country people who've provided the recipes for this book ate it as a meatless entrée on Christmas Eve. In Naples and the nearby seaside towns and villages, people ate spaghetti with clams on Christmas Eve, but these weren't available inland.

Another very common variant, particularly in Calabria, uses bread crumbs instead of the anchovies. The bread crumbs are added on top of the spaghetti as soon as it is put into the oil and sautéed until it is slightly crunchy. Since the spaghetti cooks in the skillet after it has been drained, be careful to drain it while it is still very *al dente*, really rather chewy, and remember that it's always a good idea to set aside a little of the cooking water before you drain the pasta.

Serves 4

4 garlic cloves, lightly crushed
a piece of fresh or pickled chile
¼ cup extra virgin olive oil
6 canned anchovies in oil

13oz (400g) vermicelli (like spaghetti,
*   but slightly thicker)*
1 tbsp chopped parsley

Gently fry the garlic and chile, varying the quantity according to taste, in the olive oil until they are golden brown. It is very important not to let the garlic burn. When the garlic has begun to change color, add the anchovies. Mix them in, mashing them with a fork. Remove the garlic from the oil.

Cook the pasta in plenty of salted boiling water. Before draining it, remember to set aside a cupful of the cooking water. You can use it to moisten the pasta if it becomes too dry in the skillet. Drain the pasta while it is still *al dente* and throw it into the oil. Stir it carefully over low heat and sprinkle with chopped parsley, then serve immediately.

Linguine con calamaretti e cuori di carciofi
Linguine with baby squid and artichoke hearts

Serves 4

1 garlic clove, lightly crushed
2 tbsp extra virgin olive oil
7oz (200g) baby squid
8 cherry tomatoes, cut into pieces
12 black olives

2 artichoke hearts
12oz (350g) linguine
1 tbsp finely chopped parsley
salt and pepper

Sauté the garlic in the oil, removing it when it starts to brown. Add the squid and after a few minutes add the tomatoes. Cook for 10 minutes, then add the olives. Boil the artichoke hearts in another pan, then drain them and slice them very thinly.

Add the artichoke hearts to the squid and season with salt and pepper, then let simmer until they are done. Boil the linguine until *al dente*, then drain and add to the sauce. Stir well and sprinkle on the chopped parsley.

Vermicelli con le vongole
Vermicelli with clams

Serves 6

4lb (2kg) clams
6 garlic cloves, crushed
7 tbsp extra virgin olive oil
a pinch of chili powder
salt

1¼lb (600g) vermicelli (like spaghetti,
   but slightly thicker)
1 tbsp chopped parsley

Wash and clean the clams, checking that they aren't sandy. If they are, you will need to soak them for a few hours or more in slightly salted water until the sand has been removed from inside them. Sauté 4 of the garlic cloves in a skillet with 3 tablespoons of the oil. Add the clams, then cover and cook for a few minutes, until the clams open. Discard any that remain closed.

Remove most of the clams from their shells, leaving a few in the shell to use as a garnish. Save the cooking water, straining it carefully through a strainer. Sauté the remaining garlic and the chili powder in the rest of the oil, then add the shelled clams and cooking water, with salt to taste.

Boil the vermicelli in salted water until they are *al dente*, then drain them and add to the clams. Add half the parsley, then turn the heat up a little and mix carefully for a few minutes. Garnish with the clams in their shells which you set aside, then sprinkle with the remaining parsley and serve immediately.

Rigatoni tonno e piselli
Rigatoni with tuna and peas

Serves 4

1 small onion, finely chopped
1 garlic clove, crushed
3 tbsp extra virgin olive oil
1½ cups peas, shelled
8oz (250g) canned tuna in oil

10oz (300g) passata
12oz (350g) rigatoni (short ribbed
  pasta tubes)
1 tbsp chopped parsley
salt and pepper

Make a *soffritto* by sautéing the onion and garlic in the oil. When the onion starts to brown, add the peas and a little water. Fry it all, taking care that it does not burn, adding a little more water if needed. Stir in the tuna, adding the passata soon after. Simmer for about a half-hour over low heat. Season with salt and pepper.

Meanwhile boil the pasta until it is *al dente*, then drain it and add it to the tomato sauce. Mix it all together, then sprinkle with parsley and serve immediately.

Pasta fredda alla sorrentina
Cold pasta alla sorrentina

This pasta is very quick and easy to prepare. It is ideal for lunch or dinner in summer, when you don't have time to slave over a hot stove or you just don't feel like it and you want to eat something cold.

Serves 4

2 ripe tomatoes
10oz (300g) mozzarella cheese
8–10 basil leaves

olive oil
13oz (400g) short pasta or spaghetti
salt and pepper

Cut the tomatoes and mozzarella into cubes, then tear up the basil and put it all into a salad bowl. Season with salt and pepper and dress with olive oil, then let stand for about an hour.

Cook the pasta in plenty of salted boiling water. When the pasta is ready, drain it and put it into the salad bowl with the tomatoes and mozzarella. Mix well. If you like, you can also add a little oregano and 2 chopped garlic cloves.

Dishes using egg pasta

Out of a love of tradition, I have described how to make your own homemade pasta on pages 27–29. Now that there are so many stores that make and sell egg pasta, however, I realize that these directions will probably be used only by real enthusiasts. Still, more than once I've come across people, usually foreign professionals, who have told me that they were happy to spend a few hours making pasta with their own hands in the kitchen, without even using modern equipment to knead, roll, and shape the dough. I leave it to you to choose which path to take—whether to buy ready-made egg pasta or make your own. Here are the best recipes to use with it, ones that have found their way into our family recipe book quite recently.

Cannelloni con bietina in salsa di funghi porcini

Cannelloni with chard in cep sauce

Serves 4

*12 3½ x 6 in (8 x 15cm) squares of homemade egg
    pasta (see pages 27–29) or 12 ready-made
    cannelloni tubes*

For the filling

*3lb (1.4kg) bietina—leafy chard with a thin
    greenish stem (If it isn't available, substitute
    with spinach)*

4 tbsp olive oil

½ small onion, chopped

13oz (400g) ground beef

3½oz (100g) mortadella, finely chopped

2 eggs, beaten

4 tbsp grated Parmesan cheese

*12oz (350g) béchamel sauce, see page 152 or
    buy ready-made*

salt

For the cep sauce

1 medium onion, chopped

1 celery stalk, chopped

1 medium carrot, chopped

5 tbsp olive oil

1¼oz (30g) dried porcini mushrooms

½ cup red wine

1lb (500g) passata

1 bunch of fresh basil

a pinch of nutmeg

3 tbsp grated Parmesan cheese

salt and pepper or chili powder, as preferred

There are three stages in preparing these cannelloni if you are using homemade pasta—making the egg pasta, making the filling, and making the cep sauce. First make the pasta and set aside.

To make the filling, clean the chard and boil it in salted water until cooked through. Drain it, squeezing it against a strainer or colander with a spoon until it is as dry as possible, then sauté it with 2 tablespoons of the oil for 5 minutes. Remove the pan from the heat and transfer the chard to a large bowl. Sauté the onion and ground beef in the remaining oil for about 15 minutes. Once it is ready, add a pinch of salt and add it to the bowl of chard. Now add the mortadella, beaten eggs, and Parmesan. Stir the mixture, adding more salt to taste if needed. Now make the béchamel sauce and set aside.

Immerse your squares of egg pasta in salted boiling water for a few minutes, then cool them immediately in salted cold water in another pan. Put them on a dish towel to dry. Arrange all the squares on a counter and brush béchamel sauce onto them, then place a little of the meat filling you have just made in the middle of each one. Roll each square to form a cylinder that is open at both ends, with the filling inside. If you are using ready-made cannelloni, just fill the tubes.

Now make the cep sauce. Sauté the onion, celery, and carrot in the oil. Meanwhile, put the dried mushrooms in warm water to soften, then wash them, break them into pieces, and add them to the pan. When the onion starts to brown, pour the red wine over it, letting it evaporate for 5 minutes without a lid on, then add the passata, basil, and nutmeg. Season with salt and pepper or chili powder and let simmer on low heat for 30 minutes.

Next, assemble the dish: spread a layer of the cep sauce on the bottom of an ovenproof dish, then a layer of béchamel sauce, and finally arrange some cannelloni on top of this. Continue in the same way with more layers of cep sauce, béchamel, and cannelloni, until you have used all the cannelloni. Cover with the sauce and béchamel, then sprinkle the Parmesan on top and bake it in the oven at 400°F (200°C) for 15 minutes. If you are using ready-made cannelloni, follow the cooking directions given on the package.

Agnolotti di melanzane al pomodoro e basilico

Eggplant agnolotti with tomatoes and basil

It seems that agnolotti are named after a cook called Angelotto, who was employed at the court of the Marquis of Monferrato in about 1798. Many towns claim to be the birthplace of this filled pasta from the north. Anyway, agnolotti are now cooked all over Italy in various versions and with different names: tortellini, ravioli, cappelletti, or cappellacci.

The version of agnolotti that has found its way into our recipe book has a distinctly Neapolitan character. It's a recipe for agnolotti with eggplants, a dish for special occasions, which is bound to make a great impression.

Serves 6

For the filling

> *1lb (500g) eggplants*
> *4 tbsp grated Parmesan cheese*
> *2 eggs*
> *1 tbsp chopped parsley*
> *3½oz (100g) cooked ham, coarsely chopped*
> *3½oz (100g) mortadella, coarsely chopped*
> *bread crumbs, as needed*
> *salt and pepper*

For the pasta dough

> *5 eggs*
> *1lb (500g) type "0" pasta flour*
> *a pinch of salt*
> *1 tsp extra virgin olive oil*

For the sauce

> *1 medium onion, chopped*
> *3 tbsp extra virgin olive oil*
> *13oz (400g) passata*
> *5 basil leaves*
> *salt and pepper*

To make the sauce, sauté the onion in the oil. When it begins to brown, add the passata, basil, and salt and pepper, then simmer over low to moderate heat for 40 minutes.

Now make the filling: wash the eggplants, then cut them into ¼in (5mm) slices and roast in the oven at 475°F (250°C) for 15 minutes.

Process them in a food processor. Next, add the Parmesan, eggs, parsley, cooked ham, and mortadella, then season with salt and pepper and process again. If you don't have a food processor, you can use a mincer or chop the eggplants and meat very finely with a knife. If the mixture is too soft, add a small quantity of bread crumbs.

Make and roll out the pasta dough as described on pages 27–29, and cut it into 2in (5cm) squares. Place a little of the filling in the middle of each square and fold it in half to form a triangle, or put a second square of pasta on top of the first to make ravioli. The size of the pasta squares can be varied according to taste. When you have finished making the agnolotti, check carefully that the edges are very well sealed, so the filling won't come out while they are being cooked.

Cook the agnolotti for a few minutes in a large pan of salted boiling water, then drain and eat with the tomato sauce, a sprinkling of torn basil leaves, and some Parmesan.

Tagliolini, fettuccine and tagliatelle

These are special types of pasta too, particularly when they are made by hand, and they make an excellent pasta course for any occasion. The only difference between these long strips of pasta is their width: tagliatelle are ½in (1cm) wide, fettucine are ¼in (5mm) wide and tagliolini, are just fractions of an inch (a few millimeters) wide.

The different widths suit the different ways of eating them. Tagliatelle go very well with ragù and any sort of tomato-based sauce; fettuccine are more suitable for white sauces made with cream, béchamel, butter, and so on, while tagliolini are usually eaten in broth or soups, although they are also good with light sauces, or made into a sort of soufflé.

Soufflé di tagliolini
Tagliolini soufflé

Tagliolini are usually eaten in broth, but here is a way of cooking them without it. Tagliolini soufflé is very delicate and tasty because it's light and crispy. It can also be made and served in small earthenware ramekins instead of a single soufflé dish, which has the advantage of providing ready-made servings. If you use ramekins, don't forget that each of them needs to be lined with butter and a sprinkling of bread crumbs.

Serves 4

1 knob of butter
1 tbsp grated bread
3 cups thinly sliced white mushrooms
1 garlic clove, crushed
1 tbsp extra virgin olive oil
grated Parmesan cheese, for dusting
a splash of white wine

generous 2 cups béchamel sauce (see page 152 or buy ready-made)
3 eggs, separated
5oz (150g) Emmenthal cheese, grated
3½oz (100g) cooked ham, cut into strips
12oz (350g) tagliolini
salt and pepper

Butter a soufflé dish or 4 ramekins and sprinkle grated bread over the butter. Clean the mushrooms and sauté them with the garlic in the olive oil for 5 minutes. Season with salt and pepper and pour a little white wine over them, then let the pan stand on the heat for 5 minutes.

Now make the béchamel sauce. If you have bought it ready-made, heat it up. When it is hot but not boiling, add the egg yolks (setting the whites aside), grated Emmenthal, ham, and fried mushrooms. Beat the egg whites until they are stiff, then fold them into the mixture using a wooden spoon.

Immerse the pasta in salted boiling water for 2 minutes, then stir it gently into the sauce. Put the mixture into the soufflé dish or ramekins and dust with Parmesan, then bake in the oven at 350°F (180°C) for 30 minutes.

Tagliolini al limone
Lemon tagliolini

Serves 4

½ stick (2oz, 50g) butter
1 cup crème fraîche (or sour cream)
a pinch of white pepper
grated rind of 2 medium, unwaxed lemons

13oz (400g) tagliolini
generous ¼ cup grated Parmesan cheese
salt

Melt the butter in a large pan, then add the crème fraîche, pepper, and grated lemon rind and let this boil for 10 minutes. Season with salt and a little more pepper to taste.

Boil the pasta in salted water, draining it while it is still *al dente*, but reserving a little of the cooking water. Stir the pasta into the sauce, then add the Parmesan. If the dish is too dry, add a little of the reserved cooking water.

Fettuccine all'arancia di mamma Rossella
Mamma Rossella's orange fettuccine

This is a modern recipe that has already acquired a story of its own. It comes from Mamma Rosella, who is from Rome, and who loves cooking and being in her kitchen. Any dinner with a fine dish of *fettucine all'arancia* in the middle of the table is a meal to be envied. About ten years ago Tobias, a Dutch friend of mine, was lucky enough to eat Mamma Rosella's tagliatelle with orange sauce.

Well, ten years later Tobias still has very fond memories of this dish. So it's no surprise that sometimes it's asked for specially, sometimes as a personal favor.

Serves 4

13oz (400g) fettucine, best if they are homemade
  from egg pasta (see pages 27–29)
2 garlic cloves, crushed
2 tbsp extra virgin olive oil
½ stick (2oz, 50g) butter

2 sausages
3 oranges, 1 of them unwaxed
12oz (350g) passata
generous ¾ cup crème fraîche (or sour cream)
salt and pepper

First make the pasta according to the directions, if you are using homemade. Then make a *soffritto* by sautéing the garlic in the oil and butter, then add the sausages and fry for 5 minutes. Liquidize or finely grate the rind of the unwaxed orange and add it to the *soffritto*. Cook for a few minutes and in the meantime squeeze all the oranges and add the juice to the *soffritto*. Continue to cook, stirring continually, for a few minutes.

Now add the passata and simmer for at least 10 minutes. When the sauce is fairly thick, add the crème fraiche. Mix it all together and season with salt and pepper to taste. Cook the sauce over low heat for a few more minutes, then turn the heat off. Boil the pasta in salted water until it is *al dente*, then stir it into the sauce and serve hot.

Meat dishes

In the past

In the area around Caserta, peasant farmers and ordinary people mainly ate green vegetables, cereals, and beans. If a traveling fish dealer visited, they might have fresh fish, but they usually ate salted anchovies, sardines, or salt cod.

On feast days, on the other hand, they generally had meat. The animals that all but the poorest families kept for their own use were slaughtered beforehand. They ate kid, lamb, chicken, and rabbits, and if the feast day was a really special one—such as that of the village's patron saint—they bought a piece of topside for the ragù and made *soffritto* with the offal of the animals they had butchered, or some they had bought from a butcher.

I have already mentioned that in Santa Maria Valogno there was a tradition, probably of Arab origin, of eating offal soup (*zuppa di soffritto*) for breakfast on the morning of Ferragosto. This was essential, even if it was very expensive for whoever had to buy it.

An indispensable ritual

Until a few years ago, each family raised its own pig, and killed it in December or January. This was customary in peasant communities throughout Italy, and it was considered to be a very important ritual because the poor animal was made into a vast quantity of products, some of which lasted through the whole year: hams, sausages, *capocolli*, *lonza*, *coppa*, pancetta, *lardo*, and lastly *cotenne* (pork rind).

No part of the pig was left unused: even the blood was used to make *sanguinacci*, a sort of black pudding containing rice, which was sometimes sweet and sometimes spicy, depending on the traditions of each family. This is the basis of a well-known local proverb that says: "*Chi a dicembre non uccide il porco, sta tutto l'anno con il muso storto*" (He who does not kill a pig in December, spends the whole year with his nose out of joint).

Pig markets were held just about everywhere, and it is not by chance that the main square in San Clemente di Galluccio was called *Piazza Porci* (Pig Square), a very evocative name even if it wasn't exactly a romantic one.

Times are changing

Nowadays, of course, things are different. Few families raise a pig any more—only those who live in the country and still have people who are prepared to accept not only the task of raising it, but also the very sad and bloody moment when the poor animal is killed. Rosetta could not bear the slaughtering day so, as she told me, she tried to escape by hiding in the cellar.

The advantages of raising a pig for slaughter, however, were plainly too many to pass up. These days, people in the area prefer to buy meat from the butcher's to make these delicacies. It's difficult to do without treats like these when you're used to having them. Mamma Rosetta, though, prefers to get them from friends or relations who still make their own at home.

Alliances

The queen of homemade sausages and *soppresse* to eat at home is Milinella, a woman of boundless energies, whose joy and vitality are contagious. She lives with her husband, Manuele, in Sipicciano, a small village between San Clemente and Roccamonfina. They have a delightful small house behind an old church, with some cultivated land, animals, and a wood-fired bread oven that they still use. Each year, Milinella shares some of her sausages and *soppresse* with Rosetta.

Maddalena Folco, an old friend of Mamma Rosetta's, also delights us with her charcuterie, and other things besides. In this way we often receive little packets at home, containing her wonderful sausages preserved in lard, or savory pies, cakes, and pastries.

Then there's Dina, who turns up every so often with a free-range chicken, cooked (of course) *alla maniera di Dina*, for which I have given the recipe (see page 111). We get our rabbits, on the other hand, from Zia Antonietta and Zio Elio, Papino's sister and brother. Zio Elio also makes wine and an excellent olive oil, which we call *olio di Zio Elio*. Basically, that's how those who no longer have enough land or energy make the best of things. Because of the ties of family and friendship, the culinary treasures of ancient tradition are still to be found in the homes of those who remember the past with fondness.

Meat today

Something else which shows how times have changed is the increased consumption of beef. In the village of San Carlo alone, just a few miles from Sessa, four new butchers' shops have opened in the last few years along a stretch of 1640 feet (500 meters).

San Clemente, with a population of under a thousand people, has nine of them within less than 1000 yards (1 kilometer) of each other, all opened recently. Among them is Guglielmo's, which was one of the first to open. Guglielmo is a lovely man, whose kind smile and pleasant round face enriched my early life. I have many happy childhood memories in which he plays a part.

I have never asked Guglielmo how he is able to handle so much competition, which, strange as it seems, shows no sign of diminishing. So people like eating meat and have lots of recipes for it. The old dishes survive alongside more recent ones, and you will find some of the best of them here.

Capretto uova e formaggio
Kid with eggs and cheese

This is a classic recipe, cooked in Naples at Easter. Tradition has it that Easter isn't Easter without eating kid. Kid or lamb is also eaten on Easter Day in San Clemente and the other neighboring villages, cooked with cheese and eggs or baked with potatoes in the wood-fired oven. The dishes from San Clemente di Galluccio and Toraglie, a small village nearby, are particularly well known.

A great many sheep and goats are raised in the hilly area around Sessa Aurunca and Roccamonfina. For that reason, any major feast includes a dish based on lamb or kid among the many courses served as part of the lunch parties which go on until late in the afternoon. A variant of the recipe given here also includes tomatoes.

Serves 6

3lb (1.4kg) kid
3 tbsp olive oil
3 tbsp lard
1 medium onion, finely chopped
½ cup dry white wine

2lb (1kg) tender, young peas
4 eggs, beaten
generous ¼ cup grated romano cheese
generous ¼ cup grated Parmesan cheese
salt and pepper

Wash and dry the kid carefully, then cut it into pieces and brown it in a shallow pan with the oil and lard. When it begins to brown, add the onion. When the onion has softened, add the wine and let evaporate over moderate heat for 15 minutes, then turn the heat down and cook for another 30 minutes.

Taste and add salt and pepper if necessary, then add the peas. Stir and cook over low heat, adding a little hot water if necessary. When you think the peas are done, add the beaten eggs, romano, and Parmesan. Let the pan stand on the heat, stirring constantly until the eggs set, taking care that they don't stick to the bottom of the pan. Serve the kid while it's still good and hot.

Spezzatino di agnello con pomodori
Lamb and tomato casserole

Serves 4

2 garlic cloves, lightly crushed
⅓ cup olive oil
2lb (1kg) lamb, diced
1 bay leaf
a pinch of dried marjoram

1 tbsp chopped basil
¼ cup dry white wine
13oz (400g) fresh or canned tomatoes,
    cut into pieces
salt and pepper

Sauté the garlic in the oil in an earthenware casserole dish. As soon as the garlic has softened, remove it and add the meat to the casserole.

Once the meat is well browned, add salt and pepper, then the bay leaf, marjoram, and basil. Pour on the wine and let evaporate for a few minutes. Add the tomatoes and stir carefully. Cook the casserole over low heat for about an hour, adding a little water if needed. Serve hot.

Agnello al forno con patate
Roast lamb with potatoes

Kid can be cooked in the same way.

Serves 6

3lb (1.4kg) lamb
3½oz (100g) lard
5 garlic cloves, finely chopped
4 sprigs of rosemary

6 tbsp extra virgin olive oil
2lb (1kg) potatoes
salt and pepper

Wash, clean, and dry the lamb, then cut it into pieces. Place it in a casserole with the lard, garlic, sprigs of rosemary, salt, pepper, and oil. Roast in the oven at 350–400°F (180–200°C) for about an hour, basting it with the cooking fat from time to time.

After about a half-hour, cut the potatoes into pieces and add them to the casserole, then continue roasting, remembering to baste the meat frequently. When the potatoes are nearly done, turn the oven up as high as possible, so that both the meat and potatoes become golden brown in color. Serve very hot.

Braciolone di maiale
Stuffed pork

This recipe is typical of the pig-killing season. When the poor animal is slaughtered, in the middle of winter, the event is celebrated by a series of dishes featuring *"o puorco,"* as the pig is called in Neapolitan dialect.

Serves 4

1lb 10oz (800g) lean leg of pork, boned and
   in a single piece
2oz (50g) cured ham, ground
3 hard-cooked eggs, mashed with a fork
1oz (25g) pine nuts
1oz (25g) raisins
1 tbsp chopped parsley
2 garlic cloves, chopped

generous ¼ cup grated aged romano cheese
1 onion, chopped
2oz (50g) lard
¼ cup extra virgin olive oil
½ cup dry white wine
2lb (1kg) tomatoes, strained
1 sprig of basil
salt and pepper

Open the leg of pork along its side so that the two parts are still attached by ½in (1cm) of meat. Season it with salt and pepper. Make a filling from the ground ham, eggs, pine nuts, raisins, parsley, garlic, and romano, then add salt and pepper to taste and mix it all together.

Spread the filling onto the meat, taking care to leave the edges free so that the filling does not escape during cooking, then tie the two sides of the meat together tightly with kitchen string. Sauté the onion in the lard and oil in a pan, preferably an earthenware one. Once the onion has softened, add the stuffed pork and brown it. When the meat is browned, add the wine and cook until this has evaporated, then add the strained tomatoes and chopped basil.

Cook over very gentle heat for about 2 hours, turning the meat from time to time and taking care that it does not stick to the bottom of the pan. If you like, you can serve the tomato sauce this is cooked in with macaroni. If you do that, remember to leave a little sauce to serve with the meat, which you should cut into thick slices. *Braciolone di maiale* can be served with salad or with boiled potatoes dressed with olive oil, garlic, and parsley.

Fegatelli di maiale
Pork liver skewers

Serves 4

1lb (500g) pigs' liver
2 garlic cloves, sliced
bay leaves, as needed

4 tbsp extra virgin olive oil
salt
toothpicks

Cut the liver into slices ¾in (1.5cm) thick and about 3 in (7–8cm) long. Season the slices of liver with salt, then put a piece of garlic on top of them and sandwich the slices between bay leaves. Use a toothpick to secure the liver, garlic, and bay leaves and cook in the oil in a covered pan for about 10 minutes. Remove from the pan and serve.

Arrosto di maiale al latte
Roast pork in milk

Serves 4

2lb (1kg) boned loin of pork, in a single piece
6 tbsp extra virgin olive oil
½ stick (2oz, 50g) butter
3 medium onions, chopped
¼ cup dry white wine

3 cloves
black peppercorns
6 cups milk
salt

Tie the joint of pork so it keeps its shape during cooking, then place it in a shallow pan with the oil and brown it evenly over high heat. Once the meat is well browned, add the butter and onions and sauté until the onions have softened, then pour on the wine and cook until it has evaporated.

Add the cloves, peppercorns, milk, and salt, then cover the pan and let the meat cook over low heat for about 2 hours. When there is very little liquid left, remove the lid and brown the meat a little more. Slice the joint and serve it hot with the sauce it was cooked in.

Coscette di pollo al marsala
Chicken legs with Marsala

Serves 4

½ onion, chopped
1 carrot, sliced
2 garlic cloves, chopped
1 celery stalk, chopped
3 tbsp olive oil
½ stick (2oz, 50g) butter

1¼lb (600g) chicken legs
½ cup Marsala
4 canned anchovies in oil
scant ⅔ cup black olives, pitted
2 sprigs of rosemary
salt and pepper

Mix the onion, carrot, garlic, and celery and sauté them in the oil and butter. Once the vegetables have browned, add the chicken legs and cook until they have browned as well. Add the Marsala and let it evaporate.

Chop the anchovies and olives, then mix them together and add them to the chicken, together with the rosemary. Season with salt and pepper, and cook over low heat for 35 minutes, gradually adding a little water.

In all, you should add about 1 cup. Serve the chicken immediately with the gravy it was cooked in. This dish is excellent with mashed potatoes.

Petti di pollo al vino bianco
Chicken breasts with white wine

Serves 4

4 chicken breasts
all-purpose flour, for coating
¾ stick (3oz, 75g) butter

4 tbsp olive oil
½ cup dry white wine
salt and pepper

Split each chicken breast into two slices. Salt and pepper them, then sprinkle some flour on a plate and coat the chicken slices with it. Melt the butter and the oil in a pan and add the breasts, then cover the pan and cook them over low heat for about 20 minutes.

Remove the lid, then turn up the heat and sauté the chicken until it starts to brown. Sprinkle with the wine and let it evaporate, still over high heat. Turn the heat off, then cover and let rest for 5 minutes before serving.

Pollo al tegame di Dina
Dina's pot-roast chicken

Serves 4

1 chicken, weighing about 3lb (1.4kg)
1½ tbsp chopped parsley
3 sprigs of rosemary
3 garlic cloves, chopped

3 tbsp oil
chili powder, to taste
½ cup dry white wine
salt

Dina, one of Mamma Rosetta's friends, told me how she makes this excellent and very simple recipe: "Last night I started by jointing the chicken, then I flavored it with parsley, rosemary, garlic, salt, a little chili powder, some wine, and just a drop of oil because a bit of fat always comes out of the meat. I left it to marinate all night, then this morning I put it in an earthenware pot with a little oil and now it's cooking very slowly over slow heat. After about 2 hours, once it's cooked and nice and golden brown, I'll pour on some more wine and let it evaporate."

Pollo alla ciociara
Braised chicken with bell peppers and tomatoes

Serves 4

1 chicken, weighing about 2lb (1kg)
2 garlic cloves, crushed
4 tbsp olive oil
¼ cup dry white wine

10oz (300g) tomatoes
1 chile, deseeded and chopped
3 large sweet bell peppers
salt

Clean the chicken and cut it into small pieces. Sauté the garlic in the oil in a pan, then add the chicken and cook it until it begins to brown. Add the white wine and let this evaporate.

Add the tomatoes and chile. Remove the seeds from the bell peppers and cut them into strips, then add them to the pan. Add salt to taste and mix it in carefully. Cover the pan and cook for about 45 minutes.

Spezzatino di tacchino con cipolle
Braised turkey with onions

Serves 5

1½lb (750g) turkey breast meat
¼ cup milk
¼ cup olive oil
½ stick (2oz, 50g) butter

3 sage leaves
1½lb (750g) onions, finely chopped
salt and pepper

Cut the turkey into small pieces and place it in a bowl with the milk. Let rest in the refrigerator for at least 3 hours. Drain all the milk from the turkey and sauté the meat with the oil, butter, sage, and onions.

Season with salt and pepper, then cover the pan with a lid and cook over moderate heat for 45 minutes. Remove the lid and cook for an additional 10 minutes.

Involtini di tacchino coi carciofi
Turkey rolls stuffed with artichokes

Serves 4

the tender part of 4 large artichokes, including
   the stems if they are tender
2 eggs
2 tbsp grated Parmesan cheese
1 tbsp chopped parsley
1 garlic clove, finely chopped

3½oz (100g) caciocavallo or a mild or matured
   provolone cheese as preferred, cubed
4 slices of turkey breast
4 tbsp extra virgin olive oil
½ small onion, chopped
2 bay leaves
a little dry white wine
salt and pepper

Chop the tender part of the artichokes and the stems if they are tender. Place them in a bowl and mix them with the eggs, Parmesan, parsley, garlic, and salt. Add the cubed caciocavallo or provolone to the mixture. Flatten out the slices of turkey and season them with salt and pepper.

Put a little of the mixture onto each turkey slice, then wrap the meat around it and close the roll with a toothpick. Place the rolls in a pan with the oil, onion, and bay leaves. Cover with a lid and cook for 40 minutes over low heat. Five minutes before the rolls are done, remove the lid, then turn the heat up and sprinkle with the wine. Let the wine evaporate, then serve.

Arrosto con salsa di funghi
Roast beef with mushroom gravy

Serves 6

2lb (1kg) topside of beef
½ stick (2oz, 50g) butter
a pinch of freshly ground black pepper
2 sprigs of rosemary
6 tbsp olive oil
4 small onions, chopped
3 carrots, chopped

¼ cup dry white wine
1 tbsp brandy
1 stock cube
salt
10oz (300g) white mushrooms, sliced
2 garlic cloves, crushed
a pinch of dried oregano

Tie the joint of beef fairly loosely with kitchen string, but tightly enough for it to hold its shape. Soften ¼ stick (1oz, 25g) of the butter and mix it with the pepper, then rub it into the meat. Insert the sprigs of rosemary under the string tying the beef and place the meat in a casserole with 4 tablespoons of the olive oil and the rest of the butter.

Brown the meat on all sides over high heat, turning it using a spatula (or a pair of them) so that it browns evenly. If the fat shows any sign of burning, add a few spoonfuls of water. The heat needs to be high to seal the juices into the meat, which gives it a better flavor. Once the meat has browned, add the onions and carrots. When the onions have softened, pour on the wine and brandy and let them evaporate. Dissolve the stock cube in hot water, then half fill the pan with the resulting stock and season with salt and pepper.

Cover the pan with a lid, then turn down the heat and cook for 3–4 hours, turning the meat from time to time, until it is done. How long this takes will depend on how tender the meat is. To see if the beef is ready, insert a long needle into the meat—if it penetrates easily into the center of the joint, that means it's done. Transfer the meat to a carving dish or board and let stand while you make the mushroom gravy.

Pour ½ cup of hot water into the pan you cooked the meat in and put it back onto low heat. Use a wooden spoon to scrape off anything that has stuck to the base of the pan and let the water boil for a few minutes, until it has evaporated. Separately, in a skillet, sauté the mushrooms with the remaining oil, the garlic, and oregano, then add them to the gravy in the pan. Carve the meat and arrange the slices on a serving dish, then pour the mushroom gravy over them. Serve immediately, with a side dish of peas or mashed potatoes.

Rollé ripieno

Rolled beef stuffed with spinach

Serves 6

3lb (1.4kg) boneless beef, in a single piece
8oz (250g) cooked or frozen spinach
  (cooked weight)
2 sticks (8oz, 250g) butter
a pinch of nutmeg
3 tbsp grated Parmesan cheese
4 eggs
3½oz (100g) mortadella

2 garlic cloves, finely chopped
1 tbsp chopped parsley
3½oz (100g) caciocavallo cheese, grated
3 tbsp olive oil
1 large onion, sliced
stock (optional)
salt and pepper

Spread the meat out on a board, then flatten it with a meat pounder and season it with pepper. If you are using fresh spinach, wash and boil it. Place the cooked or frozen spinach in a skillet with ¼ stick (1oz, 25g) of the butter and cook it over medium heat until any surplus water has evaporated completely. Season the spinach with salt and pepper, then add a pinch of nutmeg and 1 tablespoon of the grated Parmesan. Mix well and set it aside.

Beat the eggs in a bowl, then add the spinach, the remaining Parmesan, and salt and pepper, and mix well. Pour the mixture into an oiled skillet over medium heat and fry to make a *frittata* (a flat omelet). Let the *frittata* cool, then cut it into approximately ¾in (2cm) strips. Cut the mortadella into similar-sized strips. Place the garlic, parsley, grated cheese, a pinch of pepper, and alternate strips of *frittata* and mortadella on the meat. Roll the meat tightly and tie it together with kitchen string, then place it in an earthenware pan with the olive oil and sliced onion.

Cook it on low heat for at least 2 hours, adding hot stock or water a little at a time to prevent it from drying out (you will need about generous ¾ cup in all). If you're short of time, this dish can be cooked in a pressure cooker with 4 tablespoons of oil and the sliced onion, adding stock or water to the pressure cooker until it is half way up the roll of meat. Cook it at pressure for 20 minutes.

Saltimbocca della mamma
Mamma's saltimbocca

Serves 4

8 thin slices of veal

4 tbsp extra virgin olive oil

1 cows' milk mozzarella cheese

3½oz (100g) cured ham

a knob of butter

salt and pepper

Flatten the slices of veal with a meat pounder and season them with salt and pepper. Now place them in a pan with the olive oil and cook them for a few minutes until they are brown on both sides.

Cut the mozzarella and the ham into eight slices each and put a slice of ham and a slice of mozzarella on each slice of veal. Add small dabs of butter and place them in a baking dish. Cook in the oven at 475°F (250°C) for about 5 minutes. Serve immediately.

Involtini al limone
Veal rolls with lemon

Serves 4

13oz (400g) sliced veal

2oz (50g) Parma or other cured ham, cut into
  small cubes

2oz (50g) Gruyère cheese, cut into small cubes

a handful of sage leaves

1 unwaxed lemon

½ stick (2oz, 50g) butter

1 sprig of rosemary

¼ cup dry white wine

1 stock cube

1 tsp chopped parsley

salt and pepper

Flatten the slices of meat with a meat pounder, then place a cube of ham, a cube of Gruyère, and a sage leaf on each slice. Roll the slices of meat and secure each of them with a wooden toothpick. Remove the zest from the lemon using a vegetable peeler, then squeeze the lemon. Place the *involtini* in a pan and season them with salt and pepper, then brown them with the butter, rosemary, a few more sage leaves, and the lemon juice.

Pour the wine over them and let it evaporate, then cook for 30–40 minutes, testing the rolls with a fork to see if they are done. Dissolve the stock cube in hot water and add the stock a little at a time while the rolls are cooking. Cut the lemon zest into thin strips. Before turning off the heat, add the strips of zest and chopped parsley to the pan.

Spezzatino al cognac con melanzane e champignons
Beef stew with brandy, eggplants, and mushrooms

Serves 6

1 medium onion, finely chopped
scant ½ cup extra virgin olive oil
1lb 10oz (800g) stewing beef, cubed
1 small glass of brandy
1lb (500g) eggplants

2 garlic cloves, lightly crushed
2 cups sliced white mushrooms
3½oz (100g) cured ham, cut into small cubes
salt and pepper

Using an earthenware pan if one is available, sauté the onion in half the olive oil. When it has softened, add the meat and cook it over low heat until it has browned. Cover the pan and cook over low heat for about an hour, adding a little hot water from time to time. Then add the brandy and let it evaporate.

Meanwhile, cut the eggplants into round slices, with the peel left on. Sauté the garlic in the rest of the oil with the eggplants, mushrooms, and ham. Season with salt and pepper and cook over low heat for 30 minutes, then remove the garlic and turn off the heat. Place the beef stew in a serving dish, then pour the eggplant and mushroom mixture over it and serve.

Polpettone con la ricotta
Meatloaf with ricotta

Serves 4

1lb (500g) ground beef
8oz (250g) ricotta cheese
2 eggs, 1 separated
a pinch of nutmeg
a sprig of parsley

2 tbsp grated Parmesan cheese
1 tbsp grated bread
3½oz (100g) cured ham (such as prosciutto), sliced
4 tbsp olive oil
salt and pepper

Mix the ground beef, ricotta, 1 egg yolk (set the white aside) and 1 whole egg, the nutmeg, parsley, Parmesan, grated bread, and salt and pepper together in a bowl. Once they are thoroughly mixed, shape them into an oval loaf.

Brush the loaf with the egg white to set the surface so that it doesn't break during cooking and cover it with the slices of cured ham. Put the oil in a baking dish and the put the loaf into it. Bake in the oven at 350°F (180°C) for 40 minutes. Check the meatloaf from time to time, turning and basting it as needed.

Carne alla pizzaiola

Two courses in one: pennette in ragù followed by braised beef

This is a delicious recipe that enables you to make a *sugo* for pasta at the same time as cooking the meat for the following course. Pennette are usually used for this (short tubes of pasta with a ridged surface, like penne but smaller).

The dish is called *"alla pizzaiola"* because pizza makers in Naples use this recipe for cooking meat in the wood-fired ovens where they bake their pizzas.

Serves 4

4 thin slices of beef,
  weighing 1¼lb (600g) in all
4 tbsp extra virgin olive oil
3 garlic cloves, chopped
1 tsp oregano

13oz (400g) fresh or canned tomatoes
13oz (400g) pennette
4 tbsp grated Parmesan cheese
salt and pepper

Sauté the pieces of beef in the olive oil for a couple of minutes, then sprinkle the meat with the chopped garlic and the oregano and let cook for 10 minutes, turning the meat a few times.

Now chop the tomatoes, then add them to the pan and continue cooking until the meat is completely cooked and the *sugo* has thickened a little. Season with salt and pepper, and turn off the heat. Remove the slices of meat from the *sugo* and place them on a serving dish; keep them warm while you eat the pasta and *sugo*. Cook the pasta in salted boiling water, then drain it and put it in a large bowl with the *sugo*. Stir it and sprinkle with Parmesan.

Serve the pennette immediately. The meat can be served as a second course, with boiled potatoes, sliced and dressed with olive oil, salt, garlic, and parsley.

FISH DISHES

The mobile fish dealer

San Clemente isn't a seaside village, so in the old days people couldn't eat fresh fish every day—only when the fish dealer came, twice a week, on Tuesdays and Fridays. Otherwise, they had to go to the market held every Thursday in Sessa Aurunca, the most important town in the area, where the fishermen of Formia, Gaeta and Minturno have set up their stalls for centuries.

A mobile fish dealer started selling fish in San Clemente and the other quiet villages up in the hills between the wars and people still buy their fish from one today. Repeated attempts to open a fish dealer's in San Clemente in recent years have failed. Each time the shop has had to close because people prefer to buy their fish from the van. In the village of San Carlo, about four miles (seven kilometers) from San Clemente, the fish shop that opened a few years ago is still open, but people usually go there only on Tuesdays and Fridays, which shows how deeply rooted shopping and eating habits are.

I have clear memories of the mobile fish dealer from my childhood, when I used to spend the summer months with my grandparents. As I have already mentioned, my Nonna Assunta, who was born and grew up in Gaeta, was used to eating fish every day. She got used to eating less of it, though, after she moved to San Clemente. But something she never gave up, was buying fish each time the fish dealer arrived in the village. The poor man would come up the hill on a bicycle with baskets of fish tied to its luggage rack.

Bringing the fish up wasn't a big problem in winter, but in the summer, even early in the morning, he was forced more than once to dump the fish on the roadside because it had gone off. Of course, the selection of fish available wasn't as wide as it would have been in a seaside town. He sold mullet, squid, cuttlefish, and clams, and always had some anchovies and sardines. In other, poorer villages, only anchovies and sardines were sold.

Particularly after World War II, few people could afford to buy seafood. But everybody could always afford anchovies and sardines and they could also be bought salted. Grocers sold both salted sardines and salted anchovies, which they bought in huge tubs containing 44–66 pounds (20–30 kilos) of fish. Salted sardines were much cheaper than anchovies, but also less highly valued. They are particularly salty, so poor people would eat a whole slice of bread with a single small piece of sardine, or use a whole fish to satisfy the hunger of a family of five. Salted sardines are too oily to be good with pasta.

Pieces of anchovies in oil (anchovies that were salted for at least six months and then cleaned and stored in olive oil) were also added to spaghetti with garlic, oil, and chile, as in the recipe given on page 90. This simple but very appetizing dish is traditionally eaten on Christmas Eve, together with salt cod, eels, and *capitone*, always the main components of the meat-free menu served on this night. Fresh or salted anchovies are much preferred to sardines—among other reasons, because they are less oily. Nowadays, the fish dealer has bought a van and he arrives in the village in one of those old three-wheelers with lots of boxes piled up on the back.

Improved standards of living mean that people can afford more variety in what they buy. Despite this, anchovies, fresh or preserved in oil, are still the favorite fish, so of course Mamma Rosetta's recipe book includes a particularly generous selection of recipes using them. On page 75, you will also find a recipe for mussel and tomato soup.

Anchovies

When you buy anchovies, it's essential to make sure they are fresh. Out of all the different sorts of fish, anchovies are the most damaged by being displayed on a fish dealer's stall for a long time. To check that they are fresh, you just need to see that the back of the fish is a nice dark blue color and the eyes are bright and not sunken.

The only other thing you have to do is see what they smell like. If the anchovies aren't fresh, they'll really stink. The flesh of anchovies is firmer and leaner in winter than in summer.

Alici dorate e fritte

Golden fried anchovies

Serves 4

1lb (500g) fairly large fresh anchovies
2 eggs
2 tsp chopped parsley
½ garlic clove, chopped

1 cup all-purpose flour
olive oil, for frying
1 lemon, to serve
salt

Clean and fillet the anchovies. Open them out flat, keeping the two halves attached to one another. In a bowl, beat the eggs and mix them with a little salt, the parsley, and garlic. Sprinkle some flour onto a plate. Dip the anchovies one by one into the beaten egg mixture and then into the flour.

Heat some oil in a skillet, then carefully place the anchovies into it and fry them on both sides. Remove them from the oil when they are golden. Transfer them to absorbent paper towels to remove any excess oil, then serve while they are still hot with a squeeze of lemon juice.

Scapece di alici alla cafona
Anchovies in scapece, country style

This recipe is a variant of the antipasti recipe for eggplants in scapece given on page 60.

1lb (500g) fresh anchovies
3 tbsp extra virgin olive oil
1 garlic clove, chopped

1 sprig of pennyroyal
1½ tbsp wine vinegar

Wash the anchovies. If you want to and they are big enough, you can also fillet them, but they are also good unfilleted. Place them in a skillet over medium heat with the oil, garlic, and pennyroyal.

Sprinkle them with a little water and cook with the lid on for 5 minutes. Next, add the vinegar and carry on cooking them without the lid on for an additional 5 minutes. Let the anchovies marinate for at least a day and serve them at room temperature.

Alici arrecanate
Anchovies with oregano

This recipe comes from Mamma Linuccia, a school friend of Papino's. She lived in Vigne, near Sessa Aurunca, and, like all women of a certain age with children and grandchildren, she was a veritable storehouse of practical country wisdom.

Don Vincenzo Calzetta, Mamma Linuccia's husband, owned one of the oldest olive presses in the area. He passed his knowledge and love of making olive oil to his son Gianfranco who, after working as a pilot for nearly 20 years, decided to leave it all to follow in his father's footsteps, using the traditional methods and avoiding all artificial chemicals.

Serves 6

10oz (300g) bread (use bread that is firm,
   but has not dried out completely)
4 tbsp wine vinegar
8 tbsp extra virgin olive oil

3 tbsp oregano
4 garlic cloves, chopped
2lb (1kg) fresh anchovies
salt

Slice the bread, then remove the crusts and set them aside. Crumble the soft part of the bread into a bowl, then sprinkle the vinegar, 3 tablespoons of the oil, and the oregano onto the bread crumbs. Add the garlic and mix it all together. The bread crumbs should be slightly damp but not too wet.

Clean and fillet the anchovies. Open them out flat, keeping the two halves attached to one another. Place a layer of anchovies in the base of an ovenproof dish, then salt them and cover them with a layer of bread crumbs, which can also be salted to taste. Add another layer of anchovies on top of the bread crumbs, then salt them and continue with another layer of bread crumbs and so on until all the ingredients have been used. Cut the reserved bread crusts into small pieces and scatter them over the top layer. Sprinkle the top with the remaining oil and cook in the oven at 350°F (180°C) for 15 minutes, until the bread on top is crisp.

Octopus

When you buy octopus or baby octopus, make sure it smells slightly of the sea, that there is not even the slightest hint of ammonia, and that it has bright, shiny eyes and damp flesh. Real octopus can be distinguished from other barely edible cephalopods, such as the moscardino *(Eledone moschata)* and the polpessa *(Octopus macropus)*, by their eight tentacles, each of which has two parallel lines of suckers.

Only baby octopus can be cooked immediately. Those weighing 10 oz (300g) or more need to be boiled before the rest of the cooking process. The biggest octopus—those weighing over 6lb (3kg)—need to be beaten with a rolling pin, particularly on the head, to tenderize them before boiling. Even after that they will need to be boiled for at least an hour before you can check whether the flesh has softened. It is important to boil octopus over low heat and to let it cool in the water it was cooked in. Before adding water, Mamma Rosetta makes a *soffritto* with oil, garlic, and chiles, then she adds the octopus and fills the pan with water, adding some parsley. It is delicious cooked in this way. If you are short on time, follow the same procedure, using a pressure cooker. The octopus will be ready after cooking for 15 minutes at pressure.

Polipetti all'insalata
Baby octopus salad

Serves 4

1lb (500g) baby octopus
1 lemon, sliced
scant ½ cup olive oil

1 tbsp chopped parsley
2 garlic cloves, chopped
salt

Remove the insides, the eyes, and the horny beak at the center of the tentacles, then wash them. If the octopus are fairly small—less than 4in (10cm) long—you need only remove the tentacles from the head. If they are bigger, you will have to cut them into pieces.

Place them in a fairly large pan and cook them in just enough water to cover them, with a few slices of lemon and a little salt. As soon as they are done (in 20–40 minutes, depending on how big they are), drain them and put them in a salad bowl. At least an hour before you eat them, dress them with oil, parsley, garlic, and lemon juice. Taste them for salt, adding more if needed.

Polpette di polipi
Octopus fish cakes

Serves 4

1lb (500g) octopus
2 lemons
3 slices of slightly stale bread
1 cup milk
1 tbsp olive oil, plus extra for frying

2 eggs
1 garlic clove, finely chopped
⅔ cup black olives, pitted and chopped
grated bread, for coating
salt and pepper

Remove the insides, the eyes, and the horny beak between the tentacles of the octopus and discard. Wash the octopus and cook them in boiling water with a little salt and 1 of the lemons, sliced, for about 30 minutes, depending on their size. Before draining them, ensure that they are nearly done. As soon as you have drained the octopus, chop them and put them through a mincer.

Meanwhile, soak the bread in the milk, then squeeze it out and put it in a bowl. Add 1 tablespoon of oil, the eggs, garlic, parsley, olives, salt, pepper, and ground octopus. Mix it all thoroughly. Shape it into fish cakes and coat them with grated bread. Heat some oil in a skillet and fry the fishcakes on both sides until golden. When they are done, rest them on absorbent paper towels for a few minutes to drain, then serve them hot, sprinkled with the juice of the remaining lemon and garnished with chopped parsley.

Frittura di calamari
Fried squid

F ried squid and fried mullet are the typical dishes served in trattorias around the gulf of Naples. This is simple but excellent food, the only real requirement for making it being very fresh fish. My other important advice is it's definitely better to use olive oil if you can, and you will need plenty of it. Wait until the oil is smoking before you put the fish in.

Once it's ready, the fish should be served while it's still very hot. It can be rather inconvenient if it is served as the second course of a meal because this means that whoever is cooking has to stay in the kitchen while the diners are waiting at the dinner table. Mamma Rosetta has never let the complaints of those who are left at the table affect her because, as far as she's concerned, fried squid is either eaten as soon as it's been cooked or it isn't worth eating at all. She says it would be a sin to eat it cold.

All this is a matter for discussions and arguments that bring the cook's character and dedication to good food into play. Zia Idea, Rosetta's sister, for example, sees it quite the other way. All the same, it's true that sometimes even I would prefer to eat lukewarm fried fish and have Rosetta at the table with us.

Serves 4

2lb (1 kg) squid
oil for frying, preferably olive oil
all-purpose flour, for coating

1 lemon
salt and pepper

Clean the squid and cut it into rings. Heat plenty of oil in a large skillet. Dip the rings of squid into the flour, then fry them in the boiling oil. When they are golden brown on both sides, transfer them onto some absorbent paper towels to drain. Season to taste with salt and pepper and sprinkle them with lemon juice.

Calamari farciti
Stuffed squid

Serves 4

8 medium squid, weighing 1lb 10oz (800g) in all
2 eggs
2 tbsp chopped parsley, plus extra to garnish
5 fillets of canned anchovies in oil, chopped
½ cup (2oz, 50g) grated Parmesan cheese
8oz (250g) canned tuna in oil

2 tbsp grated bread
5 tbsp extra virgin olive oil
2 garlic cloves, crushed
1 fish stock cube
½ cup dry white wine
salt and pepper

Clean the squid, then remove the tentacles and clean the insides carefully (there is usually a little sand in there), taking care not to tear them. Remove the horny beak at the center of the tentacles. Chop the tentacles finely and set them aside. Beat the eggs in a bowl and season them with salt and pepper, then add the parsley, chopped anchovies, chopped tentacles, and Parmesan.

Break the tuna into pieces and add that too. Add the grated bread and mix it all thoroughly. Stuff the squid with this mixture and close the openings with wooden toothpicks. Sauté the stuffed squid in a pan with the oil and garlic until they start to brown. Meanwhile, dissolve the fish stock cube in hot water.

When the calamari are a good golden brown color, sprinkle them with the wine and let it evaporate, then add a little hot stock and cover the pan. Cook the squid over low heat. It's important to add some stock little by little as they cook, so that they do not dry out too much or burn. Sprinkle with chopped parsley before serving.

Salt cod

The word for salt cod—*baccalà*—is derived from the Dutch *kabeljauw*, which means "cod." The technique for drying it seems to have been invented by Portuguese sailors, who called it *bacalhau*.

Nonno Antonio Lato used to buy it wholesale from a warehouse in Caserta. He bought 110 pounds (50 kilos) at a time and stored it in hessian sacks in the attic, far away from the part of the house that people lived in, because it didn't smell too good. Before cooking, salt cod needs to be soaked in a bowl of water for at least two days, and the water changed at least three times a day.

In the Caserta area, people prefer the sort known as "*baccalà* San Giovanni," which is unusually thick. In Rome, on the other hand, they sell Norwegian salt cod, which is much thinner. When Mamma Rosetta married and went to live in Rome, she found that she couldn't get on with the thin Norwegian salt cod. She got into the habit of bringing her preferred salt cod with her from her home village and keeping it in canvas sacks on the balcony outside the kitchen of her flat. Like *capitone*, which is discussed below, it is never missing from the dinner table on Christmas Eve, New Year's Eve, or Good Friday, when it is traditional to eat only fish.

Baccalà con olive e capperi
Salt cod with olives and capers

Serves 4

1¼lb (600g) pre-soaked salt cod
6 tbsp extra virgin olive oil
2 garlic cloves, crushed
scant 1 cup black olives, pitted and chopped
2oz (50g) capers, chopped

1 tsp oregano
2 ripe tomatoes, coarsely chopped
1 tbsp chopped parsley
salt and pepper

Wash the salt cod and boil it for about 10 minutes, then drain it and remove the skin and bones. Cut the fish into small pieces and sauté it in the oil with the garlic, olives, capers, and oregano. Cover the pan and cook over low heat.

After 10 minutes, add the tomatoes, then check the seasoning and add salt and pepper if necessary. Stir the mixture, then cover the pan again and let it continue cooking. Stir every so often and turn the pieces of salt cod over, adding a little water if the sauce gets too dry. After about another 15 minutes, check whether it is done. If it is, turn off the heat and sprinkle with the parsley, then let rest for 5 minutes before serving.

Capitone and other eels

These are the fish we eat at Christmas. If there is no smell of eel or *capitone* escaping from the kitchens of a Neapolitan home on Christmas Eve, it means that the people in that house aren't going to have a real Christmas. Just as panettone symbolizes modern Italian Christmases, *capitone* has always been, and still is, the symbol of Christmas in Naples.

This tradition isn't just upheld by the Neapolitans. In Sessa Aurunca, for example, the stalls selling eel and *capitone* are set up very early on the morning of Christmas Eve. The noise of shoppers attracted by the call *"O capitone ch' 'e rrecchie, 'o' capitone ch' errecchie"* begins at the same time. The fish dealers come from Formia, Minturno, and Gaeta or from the river Garigliano and they know that the market in Sessa is the most important one, where people from all the villages around come to shop. They flock to the market to buy their Christmas fish.

Ordinary eels, which we call *anguille*, are fished from rivers or wetlands, while the *capitone* is a very long, fat female eel that is fished from the sea. The *capitone*'s head has a protuberance on each side, and it's big enough to justify the name of *"capitone ch' 'e recchie,"* which means "big head with ears." The *capitone* has a better flavor but is also much more expensive than ordinary eels, which means that in the past only middle-class people could afford to buy it. The others made do with ordinary eels, which were much cheaper. Indeed, if they wanted to, they could catch some for themselves from the banks of the river Garigliano. In that way, every family, even the poorest, could celebrate Christmas Eve with a fine dish of eels cooked in various ways.

Christmas Eve

The dinner served on Christmas Eve involved a great deal more than just one dish of eels or *capitone*. On that evening, at least twelve different dishes were served, including *broccoli di rapa*, spaghetti with fish, filled fritters, and salt cod cooked in various different ways.

Then there were eels or *capitone* served stewed or roasted with bay leaves, *insalata di rinforzo* (see page 55), bread, dried fruit (usually figs stuffed with almonds), oranges, and a variety of grape that ripened in the winter, just in time for Christmas. Christmas Eve dinners have changed a lot these days.

The basic fish dishes, such as *capitone* and salt cod, are still served, but because people have more money to spend, they are accompanied by shrimp, lobsters, sea bass, and other expensive sorts of fish.

Anguille fritte con l'aceto
Fried eels with vinegar

I f you can't buy eels that have already been skinned, you will need to cut through the skin around the eel's throat, just below its head, then pull the skin down toward its tail, wearing a pair of cotton gloves. In the old days, people skinned eels and capitone by cutting around the skin under the head, then putting their hands into the ash in the fireplace so that the eel skin would not slip. To gut an eel, slice down its belly with a sharp knife, remove its guts and the coagulated blood along its bones, and finally cut off its fins and head.

This dish should be made the day before it is needed.

Serves 6

2lb (1kg) eels
all-purpose flour, for coating
oil, for frying
chili flakes, to taste
2 garlic cloves, chopped

oregano, to taste
generous ¾ cup wine vinegar
1 tbsp extra virgin olive oil
salt

Wash, skin, and clean the eels carefully and cut them into pieces, then dry them and coat them with the flour. Fry the eels in a large skillet in plenty of oil. When they are well browned, drain them and place them on absorbent paper towels. Layer the pieces of fried eel in a serving bowl, sprinkling chili flakes, garlic, oregano, and salt onto each layer.

Heat the vinegar and extra virgin olive oil in a covered pan and boil them for 2 minutes. Pour the oil and vinegar over the fried eels and let marinate for 24 hours before serving.

Capitone di Natale
Christmas capitone

Serves 6

1 fairly large capitone
¼ cup extra virgin olive oil
¼ cup white wine vinegar
2 garlic cloves, chopped

6 bay leaves
1 sprig of rosemary
1 tbsp chopped parsley
salt and pepper

Cut around the *capitone* below its head with a sharp knife and pull the skin down to remove it. Make a marinade with the oil, vinegar, salt, pepper, garlic, and bay leaves.

Cut the *capitone* into pieces and marinate it for at least an hour. Thread the pieces of *capitone* onto a spit, interspersing them with bay leaves, and broil them slowly, basting them with a sprig of rosemary dipped into the remaining marinade. When the *capitone* is done, serve it sprinkled with the chopped parsley.

Red mullet, striped bream, and more ...

Freshness, preparation, and other suggestions

To tell if a fish is fresh, check its smell, which at its strongest should be like the fragrant scent of seaweed and sea water. You should also make sure that the abdomen is smooth and unmarked. It should never be swollen and the skin must not be too taut.

The eyes should be bright and must not be sunken; the gills must be pink or red and fairly damp and shiny, and they must never be blackish in color or smell unpleasant. Check that the skin has not separated from the flesh and that it has not been torn. The scales should be compact, shiny, and attached to the skin. If you cannot arrange for the fish dealer to prepare the fish for you, you will have to start by scraping the scales off.

Lay the fish on a cutting board or marble slab, holding the tail with one hand and a knife with the other. Taking care not to exert too much pressure—so you don't break the skin and the flesh—run the knife up the fish from the tail to the head, in the opposite direction to the scales. Finally, beat the fish with the flat side of the blade to put its body back into shape. Use a pair of scissors to cut off the tail, fins, and "beard"—any protuberances above or below the mouth.

If it is a fish such as sole, which needs to be skinned, rest it on the board and cut across the skin just above the tail, using a very sharp knife. Insert your thumb between the skin and the flesh, so as to raise the edge of the skin, then little by little pull it backward toward the head. Take care not to tear it. Follow the same procedure for the other side.

To clean the inside of the fish, open its belly by making a cut from the anal orifice to the head and empty it completely. It is best to do this under running water. Finally, clean the gills, removing them if you prefer, then wash the fish. If it is a sea fish, it is best to wash it in slightly salted water. If it is a freshwater fish, wash it in fresh water with slices of lemon. Dry it. The fish is now ready to be cooked.

Sometimes the head is cut off as well, but at other times people prefer to leave the head and tail on to avoid mutilating a fish which, for example, they want to roast and serve whole. If you remove the head, remember that it can be used to make fish stock—useful for when you need to add liquid to a dish so that it doesn't become too dry or burn.

To make fish stock, so that you don't have to use plain water or a stock cube, boil an onion, some celery, a carrot, some parsley, garlic, bay leaves, and thyme in 7 cups of water with a little white wine vinegar. Cook it for 30 minutes, then pour through a strainer. If you are using sea fish, add the heads or other parts of the fish to the hot stock, then cover it and boil until they are cooked through. If you are using freshwater fish, or if you have some crustaceans or shellfish, put them into stock which is very hot, but not yet boiling. It is better not to use oily fish such as eels, mackerel, or sardines for making stock. Once the fish is cooked, let the stock rest for at least 15 minutes. If you have used parts of the fish that would otherwise have been thrown away, you will need to strain the stock again before you use it.

Grigliata di triglie alla maniera dei pescatori

Grilled red mullet fisherman's style

Serves 6

¼ cup extra virgin olive oil
3 garlic cloves, chopped
2 tbsp chopped parsley

juice of 2 lemons
6 red mullet (use red snapper or pompano)
salt and pepper

Make a marinade using the oil, garlic, parsley, lemon juice, salt, and pepper. Clean the mullet and marinate them for at least an hour. Meanwhile, heat the broiler. When the fish is ready, cook it for 5–8 minutes on each side, depending on its size. Serve immediately.

Cernia al sale

Grouper baked in a crust of salt

Serves 4

1 grouper, weighing about 2lb (1kg)
3lb (1.4kg) coarse sea salt
4 tbsp extra virgin olive oil

juice of 1 lemon
1 tbsp chopped parsley

Descale, gut, and carefully wash the grouper. Dry it thoroughly. Use a fish kettle or any other baking pan with a lid that is large enough for the fish you have bought. Put half the salt in the bottom of the fish kettle or pan, then lay the grouper on top and cover it with the rest of the salt.

Cover with the lid and bake in the oven at 400°F (200°C) for about an hour. Remove the grouper from the oven and lift off the top layer of salt, which should come away in a single piece. Remove the skin and fillet the fish, placing the fillets in a serving dish. Dress the fish with the oil, lemon juice, and parsley and serve.

Triglie al cartoccio
Red mullet baked in paper

Serves 6

6 red mullet (use red snapper or pompano),
    each weighing about 8oz (250g)
3 garlic cloves
2 tbsp chopped parsley
2 tbsp chopped mint

juice of 2 lemons
4 tbsp grated bread
7 tbsp extra virgin olive oil
salt and pepper

Clean and descale the mullet. Chop 2 of the garlic cloves and combine them with the parsley, mint, salt, pepper, and lemon juice.
    In a skillet, brown the grated bread in 4 tablespoons of oil with the remaining garlic clove, lightly crushed. When the grated bread is brown, remove the garlic and add the bread to the herb mixture. Put a little of the mixture inside each fish, spreading a little over the outside of the fish as well. Wrap each mullet in greaseproof paper, then place them in a baking pan greased with the remaining oil. Bake for 30 minutes in the oven at 350°F (180°C) and serve immediately in the paper packages.

Merluzzetti all'acqua pazza
Striped bream in crazy water

The bizarre name of this dish comes from the fishermen of Ponza, who use it for any fish dish cooked with a lot of water. In Ponza this dish is usually made with bream, but it is also very popular with sea bass. It is served with its cooking water and it isn't at all difficult to make, as well as being very tasty.

Serves 6

6 cups water
2lb (1kg) peeled tomatoes
scant ½ cup extra virgin olive oil
2 garlic cloves, crushed
a piece of red chile

2 tbsp oregano
6 bream (or sea bass), each weighing
    about 8oz (250g)
3 tbsp chopped parsley
salt

Use a pan or fish kettle big enough to contain the bream. In it, boil together the water, tomatoes, oil, garlic cloves, chile, oregano, and salt. After about 20 minutes, add the bream and cook them for 15 minutes. Shortly before you turn off the heat, add the parsley, then serve the fish with the cooking water.

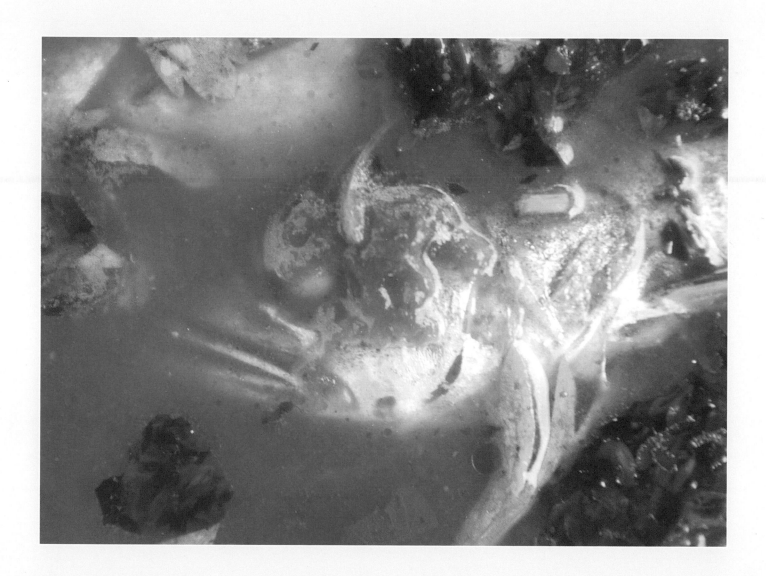

Trote agli aromi
Trout with herbs

Serves 4

4 trout, each weighing 10oz (300g)
1 garlic clove
8 sage leaves
2 sprigs of rosemary
a pinch of fennel seeds
a pinch of thyme

3 tbsp lemon juice
3 tbsp dry white wine
5 tbsp extra virgin olive oil
1 tbsp chopped parsley
salt and pepper

Clean the trout and season their insides with salt and pepper, then place them in a baking pan. Finely chop the garlic, sage leaves, and rosemary together. Put the chopped herbs into a bowl, adding the fennel seeds, thyme, lemon juice, wine, salt, pepper, and olive oil, and mix well.

Pour the mixture over the trout and bake in the oven at 425°F (220°C) for about 15 minutes. Sprinkle with chopped parsley just before serving.

VEGETABLES

Mamma Rosetta always uses seasonal vegetables to make her side dishes. She is very strict about this and it goes back to the principles of country cooking, according to which it is unthinkable to eat fresh eggplants in December, or green beans and fennel all year round. Those who are in touch with the soil believe that out-of-season vegetables, as well as being less tasty and good to eat, are also less nutritious because they couldn't have been grown without chemicals. They are rightly convinced that Mother Nature is so boundlessly wise that she has specific reasons for giving us the right foods, containing the right amount of calories, vitamins, and so on at each time of the year. It could be objected that no one really wants to eat artichokes or beans day after day for two months on end. If you're clever enough to cook the vegetables in a different way each day, though, the problem is solved.

Trying to decide which recipes to include in this chapter of the book, I was struck by the number of dishes invented for each type of vegetable. I had rarely come across such a range of dishes all based on eggplants, tomatoes, or bell peppers. The recipes are so varied and imaginative because of the need to cook the vegetables in enough different ways for the family not to get bored with them. The dishes in this chapter are just a few selected from a great many that could fill a whole book by themselves.

Many of the recipes included in this chapter are excellent as side dishes, others as antipasti (such as the ones for stuffed tomatoes). Others, such as the artichokes, stuffed eggplants, and *ciambotta*, can be served as entrées, since they are substantial and nutritious enough to make a light meal by themselves. In short, there's something for all tastes and every need.

Sfornato di asparagi e piselli

Asparagus and pea bake

Serves 6

2lb (1kg) asparagus
1½ cups shelled peas
½ stick (2oz, 50g) butter
4 eggs
⅓ cup all-purpose flour

¼ cup milk
3½oz (100g) cooked ham, chopped
½ cup grated Gruyère cheese
grated bread, for coating
salt

Scrape the asparagus and wash it carefully, then cut off and discard the white part of the stems and cut the edible part into small pieces. Cook the peas in salted boiling water for about 10 minutes, then drain them and set them aside. Beat ½ stick (2oz, 50g) of the butter in a bowl with a wooden spoon until it is light and creamy. Add the eggs one at a time, then the flour, mixing thoroughly until all the ingredients are incorporated. Pour in the milk and add the asparagus, peas, ham, and Gruyère. Season with a pinch of salt.

Grease a cake pan with the remaining butter, sprinkle it with grated bread and pour in the mixture. Level the top, then cook it in the oven at 350°F (180°C) for about an hour. When you remove the bake from the oven, let it cool a little before turning it out onto a serving dish. The bake can also be served cold. It is excellent as an antipasto or as an entrée.

Frittata con la verdura

Swiss chard or spinach omelet

Serves 5

2lb 10oz (1.2kg) swiss chard or spinach
6 tbsp extra virgin olive oil
a small piece of chile
2 garlic cloves, crushed

4 eggs
1¼ cups grated Parmesan cheese
1 tbsp grated bread
salt and pepper

Cook the swiss chard or spinach in salted boiling water, then drain it, squeezing it well. Chop it and sauté it in a skillet with 3 tablespoons of the oil, the piece of chile, and the garlic. Stir, cooking until any water from the vegetables has been completely absorbed. Beat the eggs with salt and pepper in a bowl, then add the Parmesan and then the vegetables. Mix thoroughly.

Heat 2 tablespoons of the oil in a nonstick skillet. Add the egg-and-vegetable mixture, then sprinkle it with half the grated bread and cook it, lifting the sides as you would for any omelet. Don't fold it over like a French omelet, but turn the whole frittata over completely, like a Spanish tortilla. To do this, slide the half-cooked omelet onto a large flat plate, then heat the remaining oil in the skillet and put the frittata in the other way up.

Once you have turned it, sprinkle the rest of the grated bread on the other side. Turn it a few more times until both sides are well browned. Remove it from the heat and drain it on absorbent paper towels, then serve. It is excellent either hot or cold and is also good as an antipasto.

Cavolfiori con le olive
Cauliflower with olives

Serves 4

1 medium cauliflower
¼ cup extra virgin olive oil
2 garlic cloves, crushed

chili powder
½ cup black olives, pitted
salt

Wash the cauliflower and discard the stem, then divide it into florets. Sauté it gently with the oil, garlic, and a pinch of chili powder. Cover it with a lid and cook over low heat for about 10 minutes.

When the cauliflower is nearly done, add the olives and season it with salt, then continue to cook it for a few more minutes without the lid, stirring from time to time to keep it from sticking.

Cicoria pazza
Chicory with chile

Serves 4

2lb (1kg) leafy green Catalogna chicory
2 garlic cloves, crushed
1 chile, deseeded

4 tbsp extra virgin olive oil
salt

Clean and wash the chicory. Boil it for 45 minutes in plenty of lightly salted water, then drain it in a colander. If you want to reduce the bitter taste, run it under the cold faucet straightaway, then squeeze it dry.

Sauté the garlic and chile in a skillet with the oil. After a few minutes, add the chicory, tossing it in the oil. Check the seasoning and add salt if needed. Cook for another 15 minutes, stirring it frequently.

Ciambotta

This dish, which is very similar to the Sicilian *caponata*, is a delicious mixture of various vegetables. It is very common in the towns and villages of southern Italy, where it has different names and is cooked in slightly different ways from one region to another. It is a summer dish, which is also excellent eaten at room temperature.

Serves 8

1lb 10oz (800g) eggplants
1lb 6 oz (700g) potatoes
2lb (1kg) red, green, and yellow bell peppers
3 onions, chopped
¼ cup extra virgin olive oil
1 garlic clove
7oz (200g) tomatoes, coarsely chopped

generous ½ cup black olives
2oz (50g) capers
1 pepper, choppped, or 1 fresh chile
a pinch of oregano
1 tbsp chopped basil
1 tbsp chopped parsley
salt

Cut the eggplants into slices about ½in (1cm) thick, without peeling them. Sprinkle them with salt and leave them covered with a weighed-down plate for an hour, to remove any bitterness. Peel and cube the potatoes. Remove the seeds from the bell peppers and cut them into strips.

When the eggplants are ready, wash them and squeeze them dry, then cut them into cubes. Sauté the onions in the oil in a large skillet with a lid, then add the garlic, tomatoes, olives, capers, and pepper or chile (if you are using a chile, it may be chopped or left whole). Season with salt and mix together. Let cook for a few minutes, then add the potatoes and bell peppers.

Cover the pan with a lid and cook over moderate heat for 15 minutes. Add the cubed eggplants and sprinkle on some oregano, then put the lid back on and continue cooking over moderate heat for a good half-hour, stirring from time to time. Remove the lid again and add the basil and parsley. Turn up the heat until the liquid has evaporated and then turn it off and let cool.

Carciofi ripieni
Stuffed artichokes

Serves 4

4 large or 8 small artichokes
a little lemon juice
7oz (200g) slightly stale bread
2 garlic cloves, chopped
1 tbsp chopped parsley

1 small cacciatore salami (a mildly-seasoned
   coarse-cut pure-pork salami), cut into
   small pieces
2 eggs, beaten
3 tbsp extra virgin olive oil
salt and pepper

Clean the artichokes, discarding the toughest leaves. Discard the base and the fibrous outer part of the stem, and chop the rest of the stem into small pieces. Cut off the tips of the artichoke leaves and knock them head down against a cutting board so they will open better. Place them in a bowl of water with the lemon juice.

To make the filling, cut the crusts off the bread and dampen the crumb with water, then squeeze dry and put it in a bowl with the chopped artichoke stems, garlic, parsley, salami, eggs, and salt and pepper. Mix it all together. Season the inside of each artichoke with salt, then fill with the mixture.

Place the artichokes in a casserole or pan with a little water (it should reach halfway up the artichokes), then sprinkle the olive oil over them. Cover with a lid and cook for about 30 minutes over low heat. The cooking time will depend on the quality of the artichokes. To see if they are done, try a little piece of stem or a large leaf.

Carciofi dorati e fritti

Golden fried artichokes

Serves 4

4 artichokes
a little lemon juice
2 eggs
olive or sunflower-seed oil, for frying

1 tbsp grated Parmesan cheese
5 tbsp all-purpose flour
salt and pepper

Discard the toughest artichoke leaves and slice the artichokes lengthwise, leaving at least 1in (3cm) of stem. Place the artichokes in a bowl of water with the lemon juice. Meanwhile, beat the eggs, then season them with salt and pepper and add the Parmesan. Dry the artichokes and dip each slice first into the flour and then into the beaten eggs.

Heat plenty of olive or sunflower-seed oil in a skillet. When it comes to a boil, put in the slices of artichoke and fry them until they are golden brown, then remove them from the skillet and put them on absorbent paper towels to drain off the excess oil. Serve while hot.

Insalata di fagioli

Bean salad

Serves 4

1lb (500g) fresh or canned cannellini beans
7oz (200g) canned tuna in oil, broken up
  into pieces
3 scallions, chopped
⅓ cup black olives, pitted and chopped

a splash of white wine vinegar
3 tbsp extra virgin olive oil
1 tbsp chopped parsley
salt

If using fresh beans, shell them and boil, taking care that they do not break up. When they are tender, drain them and mix them with the tuna, scallions, olives, a splash of vinegar, the oil, parsley, and salt. Mix it well to combine the flavors and put the salad in the refrigerator for a few hours before serving.

Torta di funghi
Mushroom pie

This delicious pie has been added to our family recipe book only very recently and everyone likes it very much. Since it is served at room temperature, this filled pie is excellent for parties and picnics.

For the pastry

1 cup milk
1⅔ cakes (1oz, 25g) compressed yeast or the
  equivalent quantity of active dry yeast
¼ cup olive oil
¼ cup sunflower-seed oil
1lb (500g) type "0" pasta flour
salt
beaten egg yolk, to glaze

For the filling

2lb (1kg) white mushrooms, trimmed and sliced
2 garlic cloves, crushed
3 tbsp extra virgin olive oil
1 tbsp chopped parsley
a pinch of oregano
3 eggs
8oz (250g) cows' milk mozzarella cheese,
  thinly sliced
1 cup grated Parmesan cheese
salt and pepper

First make the filling. Sauté the mushrooms and garlic in the oil. Add the parsley and oregano, then check the seasoning and add salt if needed. Cook for 5 minutes. Beat the eggs in a bowl and season with salt and pepper, then pour them over the mushrooms. Add the mozzarella and stir the mixture thoroughly.

Next, make the pastry in a large bowl. Heat the milk to blood temperature and dissolve the yeast in it. Add the oils, a pinch of salt, and the flour, then start kneading. Knead until the dough is smooth and elastic. Divide the dough into two pieces, one slightly larger than the other, then roll them out to a thickness of about ¼in (5mm).

Grease a 10in (25cm) diameter baking pan and line it with the larger piece of pastry, which should also come up over the edge of the tin. Pour in the mushroom mixture and level it, then cover it with the second, smaller piece of pastry. Dip your fingertips in water and use them to crimp the edges, which need to be sealed carefully.

Brush the top of the pie with the beaten egg yolk and bake in the oven at 400°F (200°C) for 35–40 minutes. The pie is ready when the pastry is golden brown on the top and the base.

Involtini di verza
Stuffed cabbage leaves

Serves 4

8 large savoy cabbage leaves
10oz (300g) slightly stale bread crumbs
a little milk
3 garlic cloves, chopped
20 black olives, pitted and chopped

10 capers, chopped
1 tbsp chopped parsley
8 canned anchovies, chopped
5 tbsp extra virgin olive oil
salt and pepper

Wash the cabbage leaves and parboil them. Dry the leaves and open them out, then place them on a counter and season them with salt.

Wet the bread crumbs with the milk, then squeeze them dry and put them in a bowl. Add the garlic, olives, capers, parsley, anchovies, and 3 tablespoons of the oil. Check the seasoning and add salt if needed, and some pepper, then mix thoroughly until all the ingredients are incorporated.

Place a little of the filling on each leaf, then roll it up. Grease a baking pan with the remaining oil, then put the stuffed leaves in it and sprinkle on a little water. Bake in the oven at 400°F (200°C) for 20 minutes.

Melanzane a fungitiello
Eggplants with tomatoes and red wine

Serves 4

1lb (500g) eggplants
2 ripe medium tomatoes
2 tbsp olive oil

red wine
1 tbsp grated Parmesan cheese
salt

Wash the eggplants and cut them into long ½in (1cm) wide strips, without peeling them. Put them into a container with some salt and place them under a weight to remove any moisture and bitterness. You can do this by covering them with a plate with a pan of water on top of it.

After about an hour, rinse the eggplants and squeeze them dry. Sauté the tomatoes and eggplants in the oil with a pinch of salt. Add a splash of red wine from time to time and cook them until the eggplants are tender. Put on a serving dish and sprinkle with the Parmesan. Serve hot or cold.

Sformato di fagiolini
Green beans in cheese sauce

Serves 4

1¼lb (600g) green beans
a pinch of nutmeg
3½oz (100g) mild Gruyère cheese, cubed
3½oz (100g) sharp Gruyère cheese, cubed
salt and pepper

For the béchamel sauce (white sauce)

½ stick (2oz, 50g) butter
⅔ cup all-purpose flour, sifted
generous 2 cups milk

Trim the beans, then boil them for about 10 minutes in lightly salted water. Drain them while they are still slightly crunchy and set aside.

Now make the béchamel sauce by melting the butter in a pan. Add the flour, then stir it into the butter and let it brown very slightly. Gradually add the milk, taking care to stir rapidly when you start adding it, so that no lumps form. Carry on stirring until the béchamel starts to thicken and comes to a gentle boil. Continue stirring vigorously for a few more minutes, then turn off the heat.

Add salt, pepper, the nutmeg, and cheese to the sauce. Stir until the cheese has melted completely, then add the beans and mix them in well. Pour it all into a buttered baking dish and bake in the oven at 350°F (180°C) for 15 minutes. This dish should have a golden-brown crust, so if one hasn't formed already put it under a hot broiler for a few minutes.

Pasticcio di finocchi
Fennel pie

Serves 4

1lb 6 oz (700g) fennel
1 tbsp extra virgin olive oil
7oz (200g) béchamel sauce (see above)
7oz (200g) cows' milk mozzarella cheese, sliced

1 cup grated Parmesan cheese
1 tbsp chopped parsley
salt and pepper

Wash and slice the fennel. Cook it for 3 minutes in salted boiling water, then drain it. Grease a baking pan with the olive oil and put the slices of fennel into it.

Cover the fennel with the béchamel sauce and add the mozzarella, Parmesan, and parsley. Taste and add more salt and pepper if needed. Bake in the oven at 350°F (180°C) for about 20 minutes, until a golden-brown crust forms. Serve immediately.

Melanzane ripiene
Stuffed eggplants

Serves 4

4 eggplants
¼ cup extra virgin olive oil
2 garlic cloves, chopped
a pinch of chili powder
1 tbsp chopped parsley
3 ripe tomatoes, coarsely chopped

7oz (200g) grated caciocavallo or chopped cows'
   milk mozzarella cheese
5oz (150g) sausage or salami, cut into pieces
2 eggs, beaten
grated bread
8 medium potatoes, peeled and sliced
salt

Cut the eggplants in half and scoop out the flesh. Cut the flesh into small pieces, then sprinkle with salt and place it in a container with a weight on top for about an hour. Sprinkle a little salt into the eggplant shells.

Rinse and squeeze out the eggplant flesh and sauté it in 3 tablespoons of oil with the garlic, chili powder, parsley, and tomatoes for about 15 minutes, then remove from the heat and add the caciocavallo or mozzarella, the sausage or salami, and the eggs. Taste the mixture before seasoning with salt, then use it to fill the eggplants.

Grease a baking pan with 3 tablespoons of oil. Place the sliced potatoes on the bottom and season them with salt, then drizzle them with a little more oil. Put the eggplants on top of the potatoes, then grate on some bread to make a crunchy topping and drizzle them with a little more oil. Bake in the oven at 350°F (180°C) for 30 minutes.

Tortino di patate e cipolle
Potato and onion pie

Serves 6

1lb 10oz (800g) potatoes
3 large onions, thinly sliced
75g (3oz) butter
3½oz (100g) speck (smoked cured ham),
   thinly sliced

1 cup grated Gruyère cheese
1 cup milk
salt and pepper

Wash the potatoes and boil them in salted water for 20 minutes. Meanwhile, gently sauté the onions in generous ¼ stick (1¼oz, 30g) of the butter until they are transparent. Cut the speck into strips ¾in (2cm) wide.

Drain the potatoes and let them cool enough so that you can peel them, then cut them into fairly thin slices. Generously butter an ovenproof dish and put a layer of potatoes into it, then a layer of strips of speck, then a layer of onions, and one of grated Gruyère, seasoning to taste as you go. Continue in this way until you have used all the ingredients, making sure that you end with a layer of potatoes and sprinkling with the last of the Gruyère.

Dab on the rest of the butter and pour on the milk. Bake in the oven at 350°F (180°C) for 30 minutes.

Involtini di peperoni al tonno
Stuffed bell pepper and tuna rolls

Serves 4

4 large red and yellow bell peppers
10oz (300g) slightly stale bread crumbs
¼ cup white wine vinegar
1 egg, beaten
1 tbsp chopped parsley
1 garlic clove, chopped
10 green olives, pitted and chopped
1 tsp plus a pinch of oregano
1 tbsp grated Parmesan cheese

7oz (200g) canned tuna in oil
2 fillets of canned anchovies in oil, chopped
5 salted capers, chopped
4 basil leaves
a pinch of chili powder
6 medium potatoes
4 tbsp extra virgin olive oil
salt

Roast the bell peppers on a glowing charcoal fire, over a gas flame using a special pan or, if neither of those is convenient, under a broiler. Once they are well charred, remove the skin and cut each bell pepper in half lengthwise, removing the stems and seeds.

To prepare the filling, soak the bread crumbs in water mixed with the vinegar, then squeeze them dry. Add the egg, parsley, garlic, olives, 1 teaspoon oregano, the Parmesan, tuna, anchovies, capers, basil, some salt, and a little chili powder, to taste. Mix until all the ingredients have been thoroughly incorporated.

Open out each halved bell pepper and season it with salt to taste, then fill it with a little of the mixture and roll it up. There is no need to use anything to keep the bell peppers closed. Place the rolled, stuffed bell peppers in a baking pan.

Peel and slice the potatoes, then cook them in salted boiling water. Drain the potatoes when they are nearly done and distribute them around and on top of the bell peppers. Drizzle with the olive oil and sprinkle with a pinch of oregano, then bake in the oven at 400°F (200°C) for 20 minutes. The rolls are excellent served hot or cold.

Patate sotto la cenere

Potatoes baked in ash

This is a modern version of the way peasant farmers used to cook potatoes by putting them into the hot ash of their wood-fired bread ovens. They can also be cooked in the ash from a wood fire in a normal fireplace, if one is available.

Serves 4

8 medium potatoes
4 fillets of canned anchovies in oil
1 garlic clove
1 tbsp capers

1 tbsp chopped parsley, plus sprigs to garnish
2 tbsp olive oil
salt

Wash the potatoes and dry them, then wrap them individually in aluminum foil and put them under the hot ashes of a wood fire. Let them cook for about an hour.

Meanwhile, coarsely chop the anchovies, garlic, and capers and mix with the chopped parsley. Remove the potatoes from the fire and let them cool for about 15 minutes, then cut them in half and scoop out the flesh, taking care not to break the skin, which will be stuffed.

Mash the potato flesh and add it to the mixture you have prepared, together with the olive oil and some salt. Fill the empty potato skins with this mixture and heat through in the oven at 350°F (180°C) for 10 minutes. Serve hot, garnished with sprigs of parsley.

Insalata di peperoni arrostiti
Roast bell pepper salad

Serves 4

2 red bell peppers	10 black olives
2 yellow bell peppers	10 green olives
3 tbsp extra virgin olive oil	5 basil leaves
a pinch of chili powder	1 tsp oregano
2 garlic cloves, peeled and halved	salt

Roast the bell peppers on a glowing charcoal fire, over a gas flame using a special pan or, if neither of those is convenient, under a broiler. Once they are well charred, remove the skin, stems, and seeds.

Cut them in half and then into narrow strips. Put them in a bowl and add the oil, chili powder, garlic, olives, basil, oregano, and salt. Mix thoroughly and serve at room temperature.

Piselli alla boscaiola
Peas with ham

Serves 4

1 medium onion, finely chopped	1lb (500g) shelled peas
4 tbsp extra virgin olive oil	1 tbsp finely chopped parsley
2oz (50g) cured ham (such as prosciutto),	pepper or chili powder
in a single piece	salt

Make a *soffritto* by sautéing the onion in the oil until it softens, then add the ham. Add ½ cup water. When it comes to a boil, add the peas and parsley, then check the seasoning and add salt and pepper or chili powder to taste. Cook over low heat until the peas are done.

Pomodori ripieni di ricotta e pinoli

Tomatoes stuffed with ricotta and pine nuts

8 red salad tomatoes
5oz (150g) ricotta cheese
12 black olives, pitted and chopped
2oz (50g) pine nuts

2oz (50g) cucumber, peeled and chopped
2 tbsp extra virgin olive oil
16 small basil leaves
salt and pepper

Wash the tomatoes and halve them horizontally, then remove the central ribs and seeds. Sprinkle salt inside the tomatoes and turn them upside down to drain.

Make the filling by mixing the ricotta, olives, pine nuts, cucumber, and oil. Season with salt and pepper. Fill each tomato with a little of the mixture. Arrange them on a serving plate and garnish each one with a small basil leaf.

Panzerotti di patate

Potato croquettes with cheese and salami

Serves 4

2lb (1kg) potatoes
4 eggs
½ cup grated Parmesan cheese
¼ cup grated romano cheese
1 garlic clove, chopped
2oz (50g) parsley, chopped

7oz (200g) salami or dry-cured sausage,
  cut into small pieces
7oz (200g) grated bread
olive oil, for frying
salt and pepper

Leave the potatoes in their skins and boil them in salted water. Let them cool, then peel and mash them. Beat 2 of the eggs and mix with the Parmesan, romano, garlic, parsley, and salami or sausage. Season with salt and pepper. Mix until all the ingredients have been incorporated to make a fairly thick mixture.

Beat the remaining eggs in a bowl and season them with salt. Have the grated bread ready in another bowl. Take a handful of the mixture and use your hands to shape it into a long cylindrical croquette, then dip it first into the eggs and then into the grated bread. Carry on doing this until all the mixture has been used up.

Fry the croquettes in boiling olive oil and remove them when they have turned golden brown. Drain them on absorbent paper towels and serve.

Zucchine con uova e formaggio
Zucchini with eggs and cheese

Serves 4

1 medium onion, thinly sliced
4 tbsp extra virgin olive oil
2lb (1kg) zucchini, cubed
3 eggs

¾ cup grated Parmesan cheese
1 tbsp chopped parsley
salt and pepper

Sauté the onion in the oil. When it has softened, add the zucchini and season with salt and pepper. Add ¼ cup water, then cover with a lid and cook over low heat.

Meanwhile, beat the eggs with a pinch of salt, the Parmesan, and parsley. As soon as the zucchini are done, add the beaten egg mixture to them and stir quickly over low heat for a few minutes. Serve immediately.

Grigliata di zucchine alla menta
Grilled zucchini with mint

Serves 4

3 or 4 zucchini
a handful of mint leaves
¼ cup extra virgin olive oil

juice of 1 lemon
salt and pepper

Wash the zucchini and trim the ends off, then slice them lengthwise into fairly thin slices. Set a few of the mint leaves aside to use as a garnish and chop the rest. Make a marinade with the oil, lemon juice, and chopped mint leaves. Season with salt and pepper.

Add the zucchini and marinate them for about 30 minutes, then remove them from the marinade and put them on a hot grill or under a preheated broiler. Cook for about 10 minutes, brushing them with the marinade from time to time. Serve them garnished with the reserved mint leaves.

Polpette di zucca

Large zucchini croquettes

Serves 4

1lb (500g) large zucchini	*5 basil leaves, chopped*
3 tbsp extra virgin olive oil	*10 small capers, halved*
1 medium onion, chopped	*5oz (150g) canned tuna in oil*
3½oz (100g) white bread	*5oz (150g) grated bread*
½ cup milk	*½ cup sunflower-seed or olive oil, for frying*
2 eggs, beaten	*pepper or chili powder*
2 tbsp grated Parmesan cheese	*salt*

Cut the large zucchini into slices, then peel it and remove the seeds. Place the slices of large zucchini in a baking pan with 1 tablespoon of the extra virgin olive oil and bake them in the oven at 400°F (200°C) for 15 minutes.

Meanwhile, sauté the onion in the remaining extra virgin olive oil until it has softened. Remove the large zucchini from the oven and mash it. Soak the bread in the milk, then squeeze it dry. Add the mashed large zucchini, onion, eggs, Parmesan, basil, capers, and tuna to the bread. Check the seasoning and add salt and pepper or chili powder to taste. Mix thoroughly and shape the mixture into medium-sized croquettes.

Coat each croquette in grated bread and fry them in boiling oil until they are golden brown. Drain them on absorbent paper towels and serve.

Pomodori ripieni di piselli e mozzarella

Tomatoes stuffed with peas and mozzarella

It's always a pleasure to see a plate of stuffed tomatoes in the middle of the table. The best-known version of this dish is definitely the one with enormous red tomatoes stuffed with rice. So many fillings can be used that it's worth experimenting with new ones; stuffed smaller tomatoes, in particular, make excellent antipasti.

Serves 6

6 large tomatoes
2 cups peas
½ small onion, chopped
5 tbsp extra virgin olive oil

1 medium mozzarella cheese, cubed
3 basil leaves
salt and pepper

Wash and dry the tomatoes, then slice the tops off three-quarters of the way up and remove the central ribs and seeds. Sprinkle salt inside the tomatoes and turn them upside down to drain. Boil the peas.

Make a *soffritto* by sautéing the onion in 3 tablespoons of oil until it is transparent, then add the peas to it and cook them over very low heat for 10 minutes so that they take on the flavor of the onion, adding a little water if they are becoming too dry. Remove the peas from the heat and add the mozzarella and basil.

Season with salt and pepper and drizzle with a little oil. Stuff the tomatoes with the pea and mozzarella mixture and place them in an oiled ovenproof dish. Bake in the oven at 350°F (180°C) for 30 minutes.

Frittelle di fiori di zucchine
Zucchini flower fritters

Not everyone realizes that zucchini flowers, with their characteristic bright yellow color, can be used to make delicious fritters. They are dipped into a fairly thin batter made of eggs, flour, and water and then fried in boiling oil. The same method can be used to make fritters of celery, cauliflower, mushrooms, or olives.

People who love zucchini flowers have also created a more refined dish, which involves stuffing the inside of each flower with pieces of mozzarella and anchovies. Zucchini flower fritters are fantastic as a side dish and also make an excellent antipasto. Some people say that zucchini flowers are a mild aphrodisiac.

Serves 4

2 eggs
1 cup water
1 cup flour

20 zucchini flowers
enough oil to half fill a skillet
salt

Separate the eggs and mix the yolks with a pinch of salt and the water. Add the flour and stir the mixture with a wooden spoon until it is smooth. Whisk the egg whites until they form soft peaks and add them to the mixture to make a creamy batter.

Wash the zucchini flowers and drain them well. Remove most of the stem from the flowers, leaving ¾in (2cm) to hold when you dip them into the batter.

Meanwhile, heat the oil in a skillet. When it is very hot, but not smoking, put in the battered zucchini flowers and fry them on both sides until they are golden brown. Transfer them to absorbent paper towels to soak up any surplus oil, then sprinkle them with salt and serve while hot.

Desserts, cakes, and cookies

When someone opened the cake pages of our family recipe book, it was a sign that a party was being planned. These recipes weren't used at any other time. Some of them, like *sosamielli* at Christmas or *pastiera* at Easter, were made only for a particular festival, so they were eaten only once a year.

The idea of making desserts for everyday lunches and dinners or baking cakes for an afternoon snack wasn't widespread, not because people didn't like sweet things, but because, at least until after World War II, they were thought of as a luxury—a little extra that not even the richest people in the village could afford. When it was time for a feast, however, they made up abundantly for the long wait.

As well as at Christmas and Easter, cakes, cookies, and pastries were made for Carnival, wedding banquets, and the feast day of the village's patron saint. Then there was birthday cake, which was also made when an honored guest was going to visit. So in the end there was no real lack of cakes and other sweet things. People had to wait for them and spent a long time looking forward to them, but some very original ones were made and enjoyed. All of them were excellent, and some were really special.

As time has passed and our way of life has changed, the way we eat has changed too. Now we have a dessert every day, and cakes and cookies for breakfast or if we take a little break in the afternoon. Because of this, recipes for apple cakes, coffee cakes, and the ring-shaped cakes called *ciambelloni* have been added to our collection. There is only one problem—they are so good to eat they don't last long enough.

Christmas cakes and cookies

The sweet things we make at Christmas are so steeped in the atmosphere of the festive season that it seems to be one of their main ingredients. That is why, once Christmas is over, we have to wait another year before Mamma Rosetta lets us enjoy them again! She spends a couple of afternoons making *struffoli*, *sosamielli*, and a hazelnut, honey, and chocolate serpent—three sweets that have to be offered as a group at Christmas.

The abundance of these good things, and the love with which they are cooked, is part of our long Christmas evenings, spent sitting around the fire or playing cards with friends and relations. The recipes I have included here are very old ones, which have survived over the centuries and come to us with very few variations.

The use of honey as a sweetener, for example, is typical of a time when sugar cane still wasn't known in Europe. Frying pastries in boiling oil or lard is also a very ancient custom, which is even found in the recipes of Apicius, writing in Rome 2000 years ago.

Struffoli
Honeyed dough balls

S*truffoli* are small balls of sweet fried pastry. They are served piled high on a plate, then drenched in a honey syrup to hold them together and decorated with colored sugar balls.

For the dough

about 2⅔ cups (13oz, 400g) type "00" flour
3 eggs
scant 2 tbsp milk
½ tsp baking powder
3 tbsp olive oil
3 tbsp superfine sugar
grated zest of 1 unwaxed lemon
1 small glass of brandy
a pinch of salt
enough oil or lard to three-quarters fill
   a skillet

For the syrup

¾ cup water (to heat with the sugar)
3 tbsp superfine sugar
1 tsp vanilla extract
2oz (50g) candied citron peel, chopped
2oz (50g) candied orange peel, chopped
zest of 1 unwaxed orange and
   1 unwaxed lemon, cut into strips
¼ cup water (to mix with the honey)
8oz (250g) honey

To decorate

3½oz (100g) colored sugar baubles

Pour the flour onto a pastry board, making a well in the middle, then put all the other ingredients for the dough (apart from the oil or lard for frying) into it. Knead until you have a soft dough, then roll it out fairly thickly. Cut strips of the rolled-out dough and shape them into little sticks about ¼in (5mm) in diameter. Slice the sticks of dough into small pieces, about ½in (1cm) long, to make lots of little cubes.

Fry the dough cubes, a few at a time, in a skillet three-quarters full of oil that is boiling but not smoking—at about 340°F (170°C). When they have turned a pale golden color, remove them from the oil and drain them on absorbent paper towels.

To make the syrup, put ¾ cup water, the sugar, vanilla extract, candied fruits, and orange and lemon zest strips into a small pan. Bring them to a boil and cook until the sugar has dissolved completely. Take the pan off the heat and remove the orange and lemon zest from the syrup.

Dissolve the honey in ¼ cup water in another container, then add it to the syrup.

Pour the sugar and honey syrup into a fairly large pan. Add the fried dough balls and cook over very low heat for 5 minutes, stirring gently and carefully with a wooden spoon and taking care not to squash the dough balls, until all the syrup has been absorbed.

Put the *struffoli* onto a round plate. Dampen your hands with a little water and arrange them in a ring with a hole in the middle. Let cool, then sprinkle them with the colored sugar balls.

Sosamielli

Honey and hazelnut cookies

These are excellent cookies, even if they are slightly unusual. Because they have so much honey in them, *sosamielli* are a little hard—you don't expect to meet such resistance when you bite into a cookie! They get softer, though, about four days after you have made them, without losing any of their delicious taste or smell.

2½lb (1.1kg) type "00" flour
2lb (1kg) chestnut honey
3 eggs

1lb (500g) hazelnuts, toasted
1¼ cups (8oz, 250g) sugar
grated zest of 2 mandarins

Put the flour on a pastry board, making a well in the middle, then put the other ingredients into it. (It is fine if the hazelnuts are whole). Mix the ingredients together with your hands until they have all been incorporated, then gather the dough into a ball. Cover it with a clean dish cloth and let stand for 12 hours.

After the dough has rested, roll it out to a thickness of just over 1in (about 3cm) and cut it into strips about 4in (10cm) wide and 14in (35cm) long. Grease a baking pan with butter, then dust it with flour and arrange the strips on it.

Bake in the oven at 240°F (115°C) for 15 minutes. Take the pan out of the oven and let the strips of cookie dough cool, then cut them diagonally into ¾in (2cm) slices. Put them back onto the baking sheet and then bake them for another 5 minutes at the same temperature. Remove from the oven and let cool.

Serpente di nocciole, miele e cioccolato

Hazelnut, honey, and chocolate serpent

This is really wonderful to eat, and it's one of the things we miss most when the festive season is over. If you want to, of course, you can make it at any time of year. It's so good and so original that it will really be noticed, so it's bound to make a successful dessert, even though it's very substantial. It's so unique that only the women of San Clemente di Galluccio make it.

While *struffoli* and *sosamielli* are also made in Naples and elsewhere in southern Italy, serpents are different. They may be connected with the ancient Oscan people, who dominated this area before even the Greeks and Romans and whose symbol was a serpent. Whether or not that is true, everyone who tries this cake falls in love with it.

For the dough

about 2 cups (10oz, 300g) type "00" flour
3 eggs
3 tbsp sugar
1 tbsp butter or lard, at room temperature
2 tbsp water

For the filling

10oz (300g) walnuts, shelled and chopped
1¼ cups (8oz, 250g) sugar
3½oz (100g) unsweetened cocoa
3½oz (100g) bittersweet chocolate, chopped
   or grated

grated zest of 1 unwaxed orange
3½oz (100g) candied citron peel
3½oz (100g) candied orange and mandarin peel
a few drops of vanilla extract
a pinch of ground cinnamon
1 tbsp liquid honey
2 tbsp rum

To decorate

2 coffee beans
liquid honey, as needed
2oz (50g) colored sugar strands

Put the flour on a pastry board and make a well in the middle, then put the eggs, sugar, butter or lard, and water into it. Knead it all as if you were kneading the dough for egg pasta (see page 29). Using a rolling pin, roll the dough out over a large piece of cotton cloth: this will make it easier to form into a roll to make the serpent. Roll it as for egg pasta, until it is ⅛in (3mm) thick.

To make the filling, put all the ingredients into a bowl and mix them, using a spoon. Spread the mixture onto the rolled-out dough, then gradually roll it up, supporting it with the cloth you rolled it out on, to form a roll of filled dough. Gather the roll at either end to form the head and tail of the serpent.

Flatten out the head, pressing the coffee beans into it to make the eyes. Arrange it in a buttered, floured baking pan and bake it in the oven at 350°F (180°C) for 35 minutes. Take the pan out of the oven and place the serpent on a serving dish, then brush it with liquid honey and decorate it with colored sugar strands.

Torta di compleanno
Birthday cake

This cake plays a part in the history of our family. Baked for birthday after birthday, it marks the progress of the life of each family member. It was also made for the Feast of Saint Anthony, on 13 June—a great feast both because of the most venerated saint, and because it was Nonno Antonio's name day.

It's also the cake that is made when an important guest is coming to lunch. Please note, though, that for Mamma Rosetta the importance of a guest isn't determined by their position in society, but by their place in her heart. The friends of those she loves are naturally considered important, even if she still hasn't met them. So when it happens that any of my friends, foreign or not, want to get to know Rosetta and her cookery, the menu will be the same as for a feast-day meal, ending with birthday cake. It's quite a lot of work, but it isn't difficult.

It's important for the sponge cake to rise well because it has to be cut horizontally into three slices, giving three layers, each of which will be filled with *crema pasticcera* or chocolate and coffee filling. The whole thing is laced with lemon syrup and rum. So it's a wonderful combination of flavors, which would certainly be best appreciated when eaten on an empty stomach or at least a half-empty one. At the end of a feast-day meal, though, only the really serious eaters have any room left for it.

For the sponge cake

5 eggs
a pinch of salt
2 tsp baking powder
1 cup (7oz, 200g) sugar
1⅓ cups (7oz, 200g) type "00" flour

For the crema pasticcera

4 egg yolks
1¾ cups (12oz, 350g) sugar
4 cups milk
1 tsp vanilla extract
scant 1¼ cups (6oz, 175g) type "00" flour
1 unwaxed lemon

For the coffee and chocolate custard

¼ cup espresso coffee
5oz (150g) bittersweet chocolate
3 eggs, separated

For pouring over the cake

2 unwaxed lemons
scant ½ cup water
1½ tbsp sugar
rum or vermouth

To make the sponge cake, break the eggs into a bowl and add the salt, then whisk them for 5 minutes. Add the sugar and carry on mixing in the same way. (No fat is used in this recipe.) Add the baking powder to the flour, then mix them gradually into the eggs. Butter and flour a round baking pan, 10½–11in (26–28cm) in diameter and 3in (7cm) deep. Pour in the cake mixture and bake in the oven at 350°F (180°C) for about 40 minutes. Take care not to open the oven door until you are sure that the cake is done. It is ready when you can see through the oven door that it has begun to separate from the sides of the pan.

Meanwhile, make the *crema pasticcera*. Mix the egg yolks with the sugar, then add the milk, vanilla, and the flour. Stir it and pour through a strainer into a pan. Peel the zest from the lemon (just the yellow part) with a vegetable peeler or a knife, then add it to the mixture in the pan. Put the pan on low heat, stirring all the time with a wooden spoon. When the mixture starts to thicken, stir it more energetically to prevent it sticking to the pan. Let it cook for 5 minutes, then discard the zest and remove from the heat.

To make the chocolate and coffee custard, pour the coffee into a bain-marie or a bowl over a pan of hot water—the water should be barely simmering and the bowl must not touch it. Break the chocolate into pieces and place it in the coffee. Once the chocolate has melted, remove it from the heat and let it cool a little, then stir in the egg yolks. Whip the egg whites to stiff peaks and fold them into the chocolate and coffee mixture using a wooden spoon, moving it gently with an upward motion.

Next make the lemon syrup for pouring over the cake. Thinly peel the zest from the lemons, then place with the water and sugar in a small pan and stir over low heat for a few minutes. Boil the syrup for 10 minutes, then remove the pan from the heat and let cool.

Use a knife with a long blade to cut the sponge horizontally into three even slices. Drizzle the part you are going to use as the base of the cake with plenty of rum or vermouth. Cover the top of the base with half of the *crema pasticcera*. Place the middle slice of the sponge cake on top of the *crema pasticcera*. Drizzle the top of the middle slice with the lemon syrup, then cover it with three-quarters of the chocolate and coffee custard.

Place the last disk of sponge cake on top of this. Drizzle the top of the cake with rum and lemon syrup, then cover it with the other half of the *crema pasticcera*. Put the remaining chocolate and coffee custard into an confectioners' syringe and use it to decorate the cake. Adjust the cake if part of it has slipped out of place, then put it into the refrigerator. We usually make this cake the day before it is to be eaten.

Dolce all'arancia
Orange cake

2 unwaxed oranges	a pinch of salt
1½ cups (10oz, 300g) sugar	2⅓ cups (12oz, 350g) type "00" flour
4 eggs, separated, plus 2 yolks	2 tsp baking powder
1¼ sticks (5oz, 150g) butter, melted and left	confectioners' sugar, for dusting
to cool a little	2oz (50g) candied orange peel, to decorate
½ cup milk	

Wash and dry the oranges, grate the zest of 1, then squeeze them both. Add the sugar to the 6 egg yolks and beat for about 5 minutes using an electric whisk, then mix in the butter, milk, salt, orange juice and zest, and finally the flour together with the baking powder. Mix well until all the ingredients have been incorporated.

Whisk the egg whites until they form stiff peaks, then fold them into the mixture using a wooden spoon with an upward motion. Pour the mixture into a buttered, floured, round pan, 11½in (28cm) in diameter, and bake in the oven at 375°F (190°C), for about 30 minutes.

Since the time it takes to bake varies a great deal depending on the oven, you can check to see if it is done by looking through the oven door to see if the cake has begun to separate from the sides of the pan. Take care not to open the oven door too early, or the cake will collapse. Serve the cake cold, dusted with confectioners' sugar and decorated with candied orange peel.

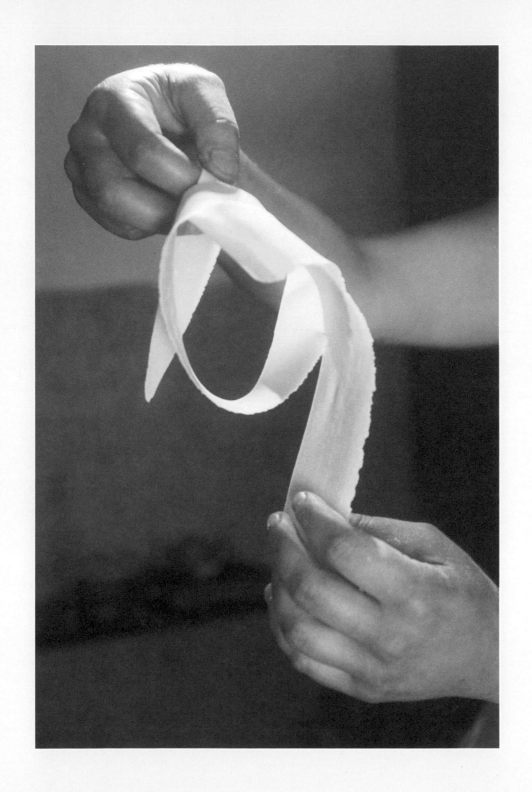

Guanti

Gloves

Each family has its own traditions. While in Mamma Rosetta's home they busied themselves making many-layered cakes that were enough by themselves to feed 10 people for a whole day, Papino's family limited itself, when it came to an important lunch, to simple, modest fritters, dusted with sugar, which had the merit of being particularly light.

Guanti, then, are nothing like the birthday cake on page 172. They take their name from their glovelike shape and are traditionally made by the country people in the villages near Sessa Aurunca. Here is how to make them.

Serves 4

about 2⅓ cups (13oz, 400g) type "00" flour
4 eggs
a pinch of salt

enough oil to three-quarters fill a skillet
¼ cup (2oz, 50g) sugar

Put the flour on a pastry board, then make a well in the middle and break the eggs into it. Add the salt and start beating the eggs with a fork, following the method for egg pasta (see page 29). When a dough has formed, knead it for 5 minutes, then roll it out very thinly using a rolling pin or a pasta machine.

Use a serrated pastry-cutter to cut strips of dough 1in (2.5cm) wide and 16in (40cm) long. Tie each strip in a very loose knot, then fry them in boiling oil. When they are slightly browned, remove them from the oil and place them on absorbent paper towels to drain. Dust them with the sugar before serving.

An Easter cake

Pizza casata

Pizza casata is made specially for Easter in the area around San Clemente, Roccamonfina, and Sessa Aurunca, so it isn't all that well known. The filling is based on rice instead of wheat and flavored with eggs, cinnamon, vanilla, and candied citron. A sweet version of egg pasta dough is used instead of unsweetened pastry. It's excellent, and once you start eating it, it's difficult to stop.

For the filling

generous 1 cup short-grain pudding rice
generous 2 cups milk
salt
5 eggs
1¼ cups (8oz, 250g) sugar
1 tsp vanilla extract
2 tbsp rum
½ stick (2oz, 50g) butter, melted
a pinch of ground cinnamon
3½oz (100g) candied citron peel, chopped
grated zest of ½ unwaxed lemon

For the dough

about 1⅓ cups (7oz, 200g) Italian "00" flour
(adjust the quantity as needed)
2 eggs
½ tsp sugar
beaten egg yolk, to glaze

Wash and boil the rice. Drain it while it is half-cooked, then finish cooking it in the milk (check the cooking time on the package), adding a pinch of salt when the milk comes to a boil. Drain the rice and let it cool in a bowl for a few hours.

Meanwhile, make the dough. Pour the flour onto a pastry board, making a well in the middle, and break the eggs into it. Add the sugar and a pinch of salt. Mix the eggs and sugar into the flour using a fork. Once the dough has started to form, knead it with your hands, as for normal dough. Use a rolling pin to roll it out fairly thinly. Cut a circle of rolled-out dough about 16in (40cm) in diameter. Keep the excess dough to one side so you can use it for decoration. Butter and flour a 14in (35cm) baking pan with sides just over 1 inch (about 3cm) high. Lie the rolled-out dough in, so that it comes up the sides and sticks out a little above them. Set the lined pan aside and prepare the filling.

Two or three hours after you have cooked the rice, add the eggs, sugar, vanilla, rum, butter, cinnamon, candied peel, lemon zest, and a pinch of salt. Mix thoroughly and pour into the lined pan. Fold the edges of the pastry toward the centre of the pan, above the rice mixture.

Cut the left-over dough into strips about ½in (1cm) wide and a little longer than the diameter of the pan. Arrange them in a lattice pattern over the top and brush with the beaten egg yolk. Bake in the oven at 400°F (200°C) for about 40 minutes, until the top is golden brown.

Ciambelloni, cakes, and desserts

The following recipes are not linked to any particular festival. They are eaten for breakfast, with a morning cup of coffee, as an afternoon snack, or whenever it seems like a good idea.

Torta al caffé
Coffee cake

1¾ sticks (7oz, 200g) butter
3 eggs
1¼ cups (8oz, 250g) sugar
¾ cup espresso coffee

2⅔ cups (12oz, 350g) type "00" flour
2 tsp baking powder
a pinch of salt
confectioners' sugar, for dusting

Melt the butter in a bain-marie or a bowl over some hot water, then let it cool, but do not let it solidify. Beat the eggs with the sugar for at least 5 minutes, then add the melted butter and continue mixing for another 5 minutes. Add the coffee, the flour mixed with the baking powder, and salt. Mix well for another 5 minutes, then pour into a buttered, floured, round cake pan, 10in (25cm) in diameter and 2½in (6cm) deep.

Bake in the oven at 350°F (180°C) for about 40 minutes. Since the time it takes to bake varies a great deal depending on the oven, you can check if it is done by looking through the oven door to see if the cake has begun to separate from the sides of the pan. Take care not to open the oven door too early, or the cake will collapse. Remove the cake from the oven and let cool. Place it on a serving dish and dust it with confectioners' sugar.

Torta di cachi
Persimmon cake

6 eggs, separated
1¼ cups (8oz, 250g) sugar
a pinch of salt
4 large ripe persimmons (also known as
   Sharon fruit or kaki), peeled and chopped

1¼ cups (8oz, 250g) type "00" flour
2 tsp baking powder
confectioners' sugar, for dusting

Beat the egg yolks with the sugar and salt. Mix in the chopped persimmon flesh. Add the flour and baking powder and mix it all until you have a creamy mixture. Whisk the egg whites to stiff peaks and fold them into the mixture. Pour it into a buttered, floured, round cake pan, 11½in (29cm) in diameter and 2in (5cm) deep, then bake in the oven at 350°F (180°C) for 40–45 minutes.

Since the time it takes to bake varies a great deal depending on the oven, you can check if it is done by looking through the oven door to see if the cake has begun to separate from the sides of the pan. Take care not to open the oven door too early, or the cake will collapse. Dust with confectioners' sugar before serving.

Torta al mascarpone
Mascarpone cake

3 eggs
1½ cups (10oz, 300g) sugar
a pinch of salt
10oz (300g) mascarpone cheese

1 tsp vanilla extract
2 cups (10oz, 300g) type "00" flour
2 tsp baking powder

Beat the eggs with the sugar and salt to make a homogenous mixture. Add the mascarpone, vanilla, flour, and baking powder. Mix it all well and place it in a buttered, floured, round pan, 10in (25cm) in diameter and at least 2in (5cm) deep. Bake in the oven at 350°F (180°C) for about 20 minutes.

Since the baking time varies a great deal depending on the oven, you can check if it is done by looking through the oven door to see if the cake has begun to separate from the sides of the pan. Take care not to open the oven door too early, or the cake will collapse.

Ciambellone semplice

A simple ring-shaped cake

This recipe comes from Nonna Elena, my friend Antonella Bigiarelli's grandmother. Antonella and I used to spend long winter afternoons studying together. When we took a break from our school books, she would cheer us up with a slice of this cake. It's the best I've ever tasted.

4 eggs
a pinch of salt
scant 1 cup (6 oz, 175g) sugar
grated zest of 1 unwaxed lemon

1¾ sticks (7oz, 200g) butter
1 cup milk
2⅔ cups (13oz, 400g) type "00" flour
2 tsp baking powder

Beat the eggs with the salt and sugar for at least 10 minutes. Melt the butter in a bain-marie or a bowl over some hot water, then let cool. Add the grated lemon zest to the egg and sugar mixture and continue beating it.

Add the butter and mix it for another few minutes, then add the milk and finally the flour mixed with the baking powder. Mix until all the ingredients are thoroughly incorporated. Grease a ring pan or savarin mold with butter and sprinkle it with flour. Pour in the cake mixture and bake in the oven at 350°F (180°C) for about 45 minutes.

Since the time it takes to bake varies a great deal depending on the oven, you can check if it is done by looking through the oven door to see if the cake has begun to separate from the sides of the pan. Take care not to open the oven door too early, or the cake will collapse. Take the cake out of the oven and let it cool in the pan. Once it has cooled, place it on a serving plate.

Freselle
Toasted roly poly cake

1⅔ cups (8oz, 250g) type "00" flour
⅓ cup (2oz, 50g) potato flour
¾ stick (3 oz, 75g) butter at room temperature,
   cut into small pieces
1 whole egg, plus 1 yolk

¼ cup (2oz, 50g) sugar
2 tsp baking powder
a pinch of salt
3 tbsp liqueur, as preferred
4 tbsp jelly, as preferred

Sift the flour and potato flour together onto a pastry board and make a well in the middle. Place the pieces of butter around the edge of the well. Place the egg, egg yolk, and sugar in the middle of the flour. Mix the eggs and sugar a little with a fork. Dissolve the baking powder and salt in the liqueur, then add them to the egg mixture.

Continue mixing with the fork. Once the mixture has begun to thicken, start mixing it with your hands, incorporating all the ingredients until you have a homogenous dough. Divide the dough in half and roll each half out with a rolling pin to make a wide strip ¾in (1.5cm) thick. Spread each strip with jelly (leaving the edges clear), then roll it up.

Grease a large baking sheet with butter and dust it with flour. Place the two rolls of dough on it and bake in the oven at 350°F (180°C) for about 30 minutes. Let the rolls of dough cool until they can be handled easily, then cut them diagonally into slices 1in (3cm) wide. Toast the slices for 5 minutes under a broiler, turning them to toast both sides.

Torta di mele a modo mio
My apple cake

3 large apples

grated zest of 1 unwaxed lemon and juice
   of ½ lemon

2oz (50g) dried figs, chopped

2oz (50g) dates, pitted and chopped

1¼oz (30g) raisins

2oz (50g) mixed almonds, walnuts, and
   hazelnuts, shelled and coarsely chopped

½ tsp ground cinnamon

¼ cup Marsala, vin santo, or rum

1¼ sticks (5oz, 150g) butter

3 eggs

a pinch of salt

4 tbsp sugar

a few drops of vanilla extract

3 tbsp milk

1 cup (5oz, 150g) type "00" flour

2 tsp baking powder

At least a few hours before making the cake, peel and slice the apples and sprinkle them with the lemon juice. Add the figs, dates, raisins, almonds, walnuts, hazelnuts, and cinnamon and mix well. Stir in the alcohol, then cover the bowl with a plate and let rest.

To make the cake, melt the butter in a bain-marie or a bowl over some hot water, then let cool. In a separate bowl, beat the eggs with a pinch of salt and the sugar. Add the butter and mix it again. Add the vanilla and grated lemon zest. Mix in the milk and then the flour together with the baking powder. Add the apple mixture and mix until all the ingredients have been incorporated, then pour the mixture into a buttered, floured, round pan, 16in (40cm) in diameter and 1½–2in (3–5cm) deep.

Bake the cake in the oven at 350°F (180°C) for about 30 minutes. Since the time it takes to bake varies a great deal depending on the oven, you can check if it is done by looking through the oven door to see if the cake has begun to separate from the sides of the pan. Take care not to open the oven door too early, or the cake will collapse.

Chestnuts

I f there is any one thing that the villages which have provided these recipes should be proud of, it's their chestnuts, which are so good that they are exported. The hills and mountains around the villages are covered in sweet chestnut forests, under the shade of which we shelter to regain our strength in the heat of summer.

I have childhood memories of picnics under the branches of these trees with all the family gathered together and long walks up the mountain where Nonno Leopoldo owned an area of chestnut forest, which had been passed down from father to son for many generations. Nonno Leopoldo was Papino's father—that is, the husband of Nonna Assunta, the one who gave the family's gold jewelry to the statue of Our Lady. Each morning, he ate roasted chestnuts and fried potatoes for breakfast—he adored them.

The chestnuts are usually stored by being threaded onto a string like a rosary or a long bracelet and then baked in the oven. That way, they keep all through the winter, which was very useful in the old days because the peasant farmers didn't usually buy fruit. These strings of chestnuts are called *"inserte"* in our local dialect. It's traditional to send them each year to relatives who have emigrated to America as a token of affection and a reminder of their roots.

Budino di castagne
Chestnut pudding

10oz (300g) chestnuts
2 tbsp confectioners' sugar
generous ¼ stick (1¼oz, 30g) butter
2 eggs, separated

Cook the chestnuts in boiling water until they are soft. Peel them and remove the thin inner skin while they are still hot and then put them through a food mill. Heat the resulting purée in a casserole, together with the confectioners' sugar and butter. Cook the purée until it is dry, stirring it with a wooden spoon, then remove the casserole from the heat and mix in the egg yolks.

Whisk the egg whites to soft peaks, then fold them very gently into the mixture using a wooden spoon, moving it with an upward motion. Avoid letting the mixture collapse—you need to incorporate as much air as possible into it. Butter a 4-cup baking dish and pour the mixture into it. Place it in a bain-marie and bake in the oven at 350°F (180°C) for about 45 minutes until the pudding has set enough to hold its shape, then turn it out onto a dish and serve.

INDEX

Acknowledgments

I would like to thank all the following people, who have helped me to transform the idea behind this book into reality:

Arend ter Horst and Peter Delahaye at the Vulcanus Foundation, Amsterdam, for their unflagging moral and financial support.

Floris Leewenberg for the photographs, Riccardo Burgio for the layout, Kate Russell for being my agent, and Barend, the director of TCS Agency, Amsterdam, for their unerring belief in me.

Jane Griffiths for her warmth, professionalism, and attention to detail in translating my manuscript.

Luca Tutino, director of Networding SAS of Rome for co-ordinating and overseeing the translation.

Su Wouda-Hanover, Peter Muts, Davie Roebers, Margriet de Koning, Ivo Cortiana, Irene Curulli, Rossana Casella, Jens Hansen, Jo Mangone, Riccardo Ficociello, and Rozanna Christodoulou, for all their time and effort

Alfredo Antonaros, Gianfranco e Elisa Calzetta, Alessandra Ritondo, Rossella Lattanzi, Milinella Torino, Zia Flavia e Fulvio Mancini, Idea Vittoria e Camillo Di Stasio, for their invaluable advice

Finally, I would like to thank Ratu Bagus and all my Balinese friends for bringing light and energy into my life and into every page of this book.

Many more people, relatives, and friends have helped me to bring this book into being. My heartfelt thanks to you all.